To Marris

Belonging

MY JOURNEY TO LOVE AND ACCEPTANCE

I hope you enjoy reading
my story & that it inspires
you to write yours.
Love & Best wishes.
M Kaipah-Mil
x.

MAGGIE KAIPAH-MILNE

First printing: 2022

ISBN-13: 978-0-9956849-4-2

Published by Butterfly House Publishing

British Cataloguing Publication Data:
A catalogue record of this book is available from The British Library.

To my grandmother, my mum
and my daughter Lonie

Contents

Foreword

When I first met Maggie, she was on a quest to find a way of moving forward in her life. She knew how she was feeling was not right for her. Anger and unhappiness were troubling her greatly. She instinctively knew this was wrong and was trying to find ways to come out of the negative place she was stuck in.

When we search, the Universe always responds by directing us towards the right people and or situations that will help us to progress to the next phase. When dealing with childhood trauma, it can be a long road to the desired destination.

We learn from every person that comes into our lives, whether family members, friends or acquaintances. During our pre-birth planning we vaguely decide on the major experiences we need to undertake to realise the desired lessons. We also make contracts with some of the members of our soul group to come and help us to accomplish these lessons. Appropriate people appear in our lives when the time is right for any specific lesson.

As Maggie began to find answers, she was led towards three different mentors at various stages of her life. With each mentor she had the courage to talk about her own situation whilst following her learning journey. From the beginning, she understood that, firstly, she had to work on herself to get out of the cycle of suffering she was going through. The starting point is always self-love and forgiveness. They are learnt by constantly watching your own thoughts and replacing any negative thoughts with positive thoughts of seeing the slightest good in any person or situation. Maggie also started practising different self-help modalities, such as yoga, meditation, chanting and, most important of all, reading spiritual books she was drawn to.

In her writing, she is incredibly open and honest about her feelings with every person and situation that affected her emotionally. She took the opportunity to examine every difficult person and situation that caused her unhappiness and anger. In short, she understood the key fact that everything happens for a reason, as she was learning from each experience. She had the courage to investigate the wisdom she gained from them.

Why did it happen? What was she supposed to learn? She was able to understand, forgive and love the people she previously thought had done wrong by her or she assumed did not love her. Yes, she did go through periods of self-loathing, coupled with constant doubt, but she knew that unseen energy was continually helping her.

During her mission to find answers she realised who we are, why we are on earth and why souls come as humans to the planet earth of duality. She learned that we are soul and human. She understood our thoughts are energy, and about the power of thought and how we create our own reality, as all our thoughts go to the Universe and affect the overall energy because we are all a part of the whole.

This knowledge has enriched her life completely, giving her the courage to face the rest of her life whatever she may endure in the future.

Ranjanie de Mel

Malawi

I am Malawi, beautiful, diverse and vibrant.
I am complicated, steeped in culture,
Deeply rooted like that mango tree.
Discontent, dishonour, suffocation,
I am fighting for freedom to release my soul.
What about me, what about my dreams?

But England, you have shaped me.
At times abused me.
Cared for me like an adopted mother
Protected me like a loving father
How could I turn my back on you?
Why would I try?

I love all of me,
I love all of me,
I love all of me,
I am peace.

Maggie Kaipah-Milne, December 2018

Acknowledgements

To my mum. Thank you for the love and courage you instilled in me to work hard and never to be told by anyone that I couldn't do anything. You showed me by example, Mum, and for that I am so grateful.

To my dad. Thank you for the chance you gave us to experience life in a new country and for everything you shared with us in order to survive. You overcame so much in your life, and I think you were well before your time.

To my grandparents. Thank you so much for the wonderful early start that you gave me. Your unconditional love instilled in me so much courage and determination to be able to reach for the stars, and I have. I want to take this opportunity to say that your input did not go unnoticed, and you are always in my heart.

To Lonie. You came into my life for 26 years only, to show me what love really could be like, given the chance. Words cannot explain the impact you have had on my life.

To James and Judith, for your continued support and many Facetime calls. James, I have always felt you knew what you came to achieve in this lifetime, and you have been relentless in pursuing your dreams. I always knew you were destined for the big world out there. I am just thankful that you chose me to be your mum for the first 18 years of your journey until you felt secure enough to take the reins yourself. I hope I did you proud, dear son, and I wish you and Judith every happiness in your lives together.

To my ex-husband, Alistair. I guess that it is with you that I learnt my most difficult lessons in this lifetime. Thank you for being there so I could experience them. I hold nothing but gratitude for you.

To my three brothers, Rabson, Paul and Peter. Thank you for agreeing to be my brothers in this lifetime. You have played your roles beautifully, pressed my buttons all these years in such a way that I have felt well held to pursue my life purpose. I thank you every day that I am alive.

To my three mentors, Juliet Glavey, Ranjanie de Mel and Monica McIntosh. You each saw something in me that needed pruning and were brave enough to stick around and watch me grow. Thank you for choosing to be my mentors on this beautiful journey called life. Words alone cannot express my gratitude to you and you are in my heart always.

To my primary and secondary school friends, Nadia Carbonari, Lyndsey Venables, Susan Hazle, Andrew Street and Karen Cowley. You have bravely travelled back to the sixties and seventies with me at my request and gallantly enjoyed the ride with me. Thank you so much, dear friends.

To Lisa Cherry. I haven't met you yet but reading your book *Soul Journey* was the catalyst that led me to believe I could write this book. Thank you, Lisa. I look forward to meeting you one of these days.

To Ellen Watts. You believed in me when I didn't believe in myself that I could write this book. Thank you for being there throughout this journey, encouraging me and instilling in me the courage that I could become a published author. Thank you, Ellen, for your kindness and generosity throughout this journey. I know now that you are an angel sent by my guides to show me the way. Also, thank you for sharing Cosmic Ordering.

To Mrs Joyce King, my 95-year-old neighbour. You contentedly listened to each chapter as it unfolded through the stages. You have no idea, Joyce, what a blessing you have been to me. Thank you.

To Maureen Raine. You were also happy every Friday evening for me to read each chapter to you as it unfolded over a bottle of red wine. Maureen, you have been my first-hand woman from day one, reading the first draft, reading the second draft as I typed it, and generally being at my beck and call whenever I needed you. I will never be able to thank you enough for your generosity and time.

To Rudy Bright and Sue McGuinness, my walking buddies. Our walks were invaluable to me through lockdown. They gave me an escape, the distraction I always looked forward to, that got me out of my bubble and out of the house. You also happily listened to me chattering on about my book each week.

To my Buddhist family in Nunhead. You have held me strong in the good times and the bad times. Thank you all for just being there for me, listening to me talk about my book, and never for one moment doubting that I could achieve my 'Human Revolution'.

The Cundall family – especially Allegra and Ottilie. It has been lovely spending time with you over the past six months of lockdown. Coming to work has been a wonderful distraction. It gave me a sense of purpose. I thoroughly enjoyed cooking delicious meals together and doing yoga, meditation, painting and chanting together. It didn't seem like work at all. Thank you so much.

To Alison Thompson, for all your hard work in turning my manuscript into a polished book. Thank you.

Tricia Keracher-Summerfield. Thank you, Tricia, for the beautiful photograph you took of me on that warm June evening in Peckham Rye that fronts my book. (tricia@portrayedphotography.co.uk).

Beta Readers. Rosalie Wright, Amie Stoebner, Anna Frijstein, Ellen Jenkins, Emma Halston, Andrea Lowe, Anne Marie Gutterage, Kelvin Kaipah, Felia Kaipah, Sandram Kaipah, Talasina Kaipah, Rabson Kaipah, Anna Kaipah, Rudy Bright, Susan Hazle, Lynn Voller, Diana Wilkins, James T Milne, Judith Garcia Obrador, Erica Vtoraja, Chikondi Liabunya, Rose Giles, Alistair Milne, Ranjanie De Mel, Monica McIntosh, Fleur Clackson, Caroline Liabunya and the women at Clean Break, who helped to shape my life at a difficult time. Thank you all for the time you generously put aside to read the first draft for me and for the feedback you gave me. I cannot thank you enough for this.

Mr Simms, The Old Sweet Shop (@mrsimms_uk), Lordship Lane, SE22. Every week you kept me supplied with my £5-worth of cough candy, which lifted my spirits during my difficult moments, and you always welcomed me with a smile. Coming to your shop every week was a lovely guilty pleasure. Thank you.

To Taofeeq at Easyprint33@gmail.com. Thank you, Tao, for your kind nature and patience. You were able to sort me out on the various occasions I turned up with a technical problem that I did not know how to deal with. You saved me many times. This book would not have materialised so smoothly without you.

To Eoghan Nolan, for taking the black and white photograph at the end of the book.

And last but not least to **Bunmi Rufai, creative**

director/designer for Sixth Sense Collections, who is the creator of the dress I am wearing on the front cover. Thank you, Bunmi, for your hard work and creative flair.

Preface

My parents did not raise us up going to church and this for me was my saving grace, because I was able to choose my own religion when I was ready. For a little girl being raised away from her culture, I was searching for somewhere to belong. I wanted to know who I was, where I came from, why I was here, and why I had been displaced. There had to be a reason. I wanted to know what love was. I just knew that there was something missing in my life and I didn't know what that was. I felt very disconnected. Finding out why I chose my parents was the starting point for beginning the journey in understanding who I am.

Consequently, I wanted to share my spiritual journey with others by writing this book. I wanted to teach others that it doesn't matter who you are or where you come from; you have the ability to change your life to be more meaningful and satisfying. The answers are all within us, but we have to be prepared to do the work that will change the course of our lives. For me, letting go of the old pain has been the most challenging thing on this journey. It was uncomfortable and unfamiliar.

Writing a book about my life was a dream I never believed would come true because I thought that only happens in books and in the movies. In order to move forward, I had to stop taking the victim stance and stop blaming others for the bad things that had happened to me.

In writing about my life, I set out to teach what I had always wanted to learn myself. I am aware that it takes a great deal of courage to do what I have achieved by writing this book. I did not fit in anywhere but kept searching. When I desperately asked Juliet, my first mentor, what book I should read to find the answer, she replied, "It is not written in any book. It is not written anywhere, but it is within us." We already have the knowledge we seek. We can tap into it whenever we want and that is the most courageous path that any of us can take, and it is a choice.

I just wanted you to know that wherever you are in your journey, do not give up. You will get there. For me, taking this journey has shown me that I am not displaced. Everything that happened in my life happened for a reason. The reason was for me to find my way home, and because I have found my way home, I am no longer heartbroken.

Chapter 1:
Anger

*"Life is about risking everything for a dream
no one can see but you."*

Anon

I wanted to write about my anger as a way of understanding it. I have been angry about my mum and my childhood for over fifty years. I still harbour a lot of that anger. I just felt that enough is enough. I didn't want her to die while I was still angry with her for something that happened more than 50 years ago. It didn't make any sense. In theory, I could understand about letting go of my anger towards her; I could understand about forgiveness, and that everything that happened between us happened for a reason; that we had made a soul contract to support each other with the lessons we wanted to learn in this lifetime. I understood on a spiritual level that I had asked her to teach me these lessons so I could fulfil my life purpose and I was helping her to fulfil hers. I knew all this stuff by heart, and backwards. I had read the books and spent years in therapy sessions; I had been to hundreds of workshops, talks and seminars about loving myself, letting go of my anger, healing my life through forgiveness and gratitude. So why was I still allowing the anger to seep through like an old lost friend that I yearned for? I would look at my pile of books (and there were many) and wonder if all the reading had been in vain. *Shall I just pack them all up and take them to the charity shop, and chase some other, more realistic dream?* I wondered.

All I ever wanted was to be happy. As a little girl growing

up in Malawi, I thought I would be happy if my mum was with me. So I knew that I was unhappy. At eighteen months, I was angry that my mum had chosen to go and live in England with my dad rather than stay with me, and I just couldn't understand why she would do that. (We were always told they had gone to England, although they were in Scotland.) I hated thinking about my mum or talking about her. As far as I was concerned, she was dead. I can't remember thinking such intense feelings about my dad, who had also left me. I was one angry child.

My childhood up to the age of eight was spent in Malawi. We – my two older brothers and me – lived with our grandparents. They had twelve children in all, my mum being the oldest, so I guess having three extra mouths to feed was nothing to them.

From time to time, Grandad would send for the photographer to come to the house to take photographs of my two brothers and me to send to our parents in England. I hated these days. We would be scrubbed clean and put in our best clothes, which our parents had sent from England. This one time – I must have been two or three – I remember screaming the place down, running away and being chased by my uncles so I could have this photograph taken. I bawled the place down. I was eventually caught and had to be pacified with a piece of bread and butter. I saw the photo recently and remembered well the history and the pain behind it.

Another time, when I was about 3 or 4 years old, Mum sent me from England this exquisite, beautiful doll with long flickering eyelashes, wearing a gorgeous dress. I was not at all impressed and I tore this doll up into bits. She was not going to pacify me that easily. I was having none of that; I wanted her to pay. I was too young to understand then that when we shut someone out of our lives for something that we feel they have done to us, it is us who suffer, because usually the other person has moved on, unaware of the emotions they have caused, leaving us stuck in our anger, unable to forgive or grow.

Every time we saw a plane flying overhead, my uncles and aunts would tell me that my parents had gone to England in an airplane like this one, and that one day they would come back for me. I didn't know what to believe. What also upset me was that my parents wrote to us through our grandfather. They didn't write to me explaining anything. This was also upsetting. It was as if, to them, I didn't exist.

A few years later, my grandfather decided to retire and move to his farm in the village. This meant he wouldn't be living in town anymore, but we children needed to be in town in order to go to school. He wrote to my parents and told them it was time for them to return home and take care of their own children. My parents were not yet ready to return to Malawi, so they decided to send for my brothers and me to go to England. So, in 1968, when I was eight years old, Paul was nine and Rabson was 11, and after many hiccups because the Malawi Government wouldn't let us go initially until we had the right papers to leave the country, we came to England to live. I was looking forward to seeing my mum again, whom I had missed very much. I imagined her saying sorry to me and that she loved me; she and I would have been the best of friends. But that is not how it panned out. I remember she hugged me and kissed me but she did not say sorry or that she loved me, so I knew from that moment on that she was not to be trusted. As far as I was concerned, she had hurt me and she was not able to acknowledge it. This gave me trust issues: I couldn't trust anyone and always expected people to let me down.

The misunderstanding between us only grew as time went on. I didn't like her telling me what to do. I would do it, but my body would resist. I thought, *Who does she think she is? She can't just come into my life and start telling me what to do.* At weekends, she made me do a lot of housework: sweeping the stairs, cleaning the bathroom and toilet, cooking, washing clothes by hand in the bathroom. She even made me wash my sheets when I wet the bed, which was a regular occurrence. My brothers were free to go out with their friends and play football.

In 1969, after we had been in England for a year, our grandad died. I remember it very well. My dad came home with the telegram during the day. He went upstairs to the bedroom, where Mum was asleep, as she worked nights. After some time, he came down and called the three of us inside and told us the news. Then he returned to work. Mum stayed upstairs. I can't remember what we kids did; I can't imagine we went back out to play, as the news sank in that we would never see our grandad again. He had been our main male role model until a year before. Mum didn't go to work that night, but the next evening, she got ready and went as if nothing had happened. Grandad wasn't talked about. I remember being really angry when Grandad died. I knew he had a brilliant brain because he could speak so many African languages. I wondered why he hadn't left me his brain, so I could be as brilliant as he was.

My mum did not tell me about periods. I learnt from my friend Ijoma, a mixed-race girl who lived on our street, when we were playing hopscotch one day. As I sat on the ground to watch her take her turn, I sprawled my legs out, showing my pants, which were bloody. She explained that I was having a period and was shocked that my mum hadn't told me about it. She went and told her mum, who told my mum. Mum was angry that she had to hear it from someone else. She had already gone to my bedroom and found the bloodied pants, which I had hidden there. She gave me some Dr White's pads to wear with a belt, which was used to hold up the pads. She said this was something I shouldn't tell the boys, and that I mustn't let boys touch me there. I also remember her being angry with me when I told her that I had ditched the cumbersome Dr White's pads for Lil-Lets, inserted inside the vagina, which my friends at school had told me about. I just did not have a good enough relationship with her for me to want to tell her anything. Most of the time I was lonely and I missed my grandmother, who had been kind and loving towards me.

My mum was very distant, and she didn't like to be challenged – which I often did. When challenged, she would lose control and shout and shout and shout, and she would not stop shouting. She would let out all the pent-up frustration that she was keeping inside. I remember I had confronted her about something when we were arranging my wedding. I can't even remember what I said, but she went off on one. I was living in London with my then fiancé, and she didn't talk to me for three weeks; that's how angry she used to get. I seemed to be the only one who would provoke her in this way. I later learnt that she and Dad were not married. They had been married in the traditional sense, in that as soon as you had a child, you were classed as married. It must have been difficult for her to watch me preparing for my wedding. I always felt there was something amiss, but I couldn't put my finger on it. My younger brother did point out that there was no photograph of their wedding anywhere around the house. They did eventually marry in the Catholic church, just before my dad died in 2009, in order that he could have a church burial. I wasn't told about the wedding. I heard about it later, and my mum never mentioned it. I did mean to ask her about it, but it was about waiting for the right time. It was all to do with timing and bringing up things in person, not on the telephone.

At 15, something happened that really hurt me and confirmed to me that I really was all alone in the world, even though I had tried so hard to fit into the fold and do everything that was expected of me. Most evenings I would babysit my baby brother as Mum worked nights and my dad and brothers would often be out. I was the one constant. I was happy to do this because I loved my brother. One particular evening I was unable to babysit him as I had promised to babysit for someone at the restaurant where I worked. Mum asked me if I would ask my friend Denise to babysit my brother; she said Denise could sleep the night in my bed. The next day, when my friend had left, I noticed that she had left her cigarettes and lighter on my bedside table. I left them there merely because they were not mine. As far as I was concerned, they could stay there until she came back for them. In the meantime, my mum saw them there and she went mad, telling my dad that I was smoking. I tried to explain that they were not my cigarettes, but belonged to my friend Denise, but they were having none of it. I couldn't believe that my own parents would prefer to assume that I was bad rather than listen to me when I was desperately trying to tell the truth. I felt so alone. Another incident that left me feeling alone also happened at this time. My parents had a guest who was visiting from Malawi. They really respected him because he had a prominent position in Malawian politics. I went into the sitting room to greet him and he touched my breast as he said how much I had grown. A little while after this, I managed to blurt out what he had done in the kitchen when all the family were there: my mum, dad and three brothers. First my mum scurried up the stairs to bed. Dad immediately followed her. And then a little later my brothers left, and I was left alone trying to make sense of what it was I had said that was wrong. Talking about it to my younger brother recently, he remembers the incident vividly, and says he was too young to do anything about it at the time. However, he swears he would not stand back and do nothing if a similar thing were to happen to his two girls.

I just remember being so lonely as a child. I couldn't talk to my brothers about my deep feelings. We were all dealing with stuff of some kind ourselves. I felt that my parents were always running, but I didn't know where they were running to. I would sometimes overhear Mum saying to people that she had lost me, and I would wonder what she meant.

When my children were born, I thought my mum would stick around and help me raise them because she hadn't been around for me. But after 30 years in England, she and Dad decided to go back to Malawi. For me, it seemed like a second abandonment. I lost myself in caring for my children as a way of hiding from the pain. My mum made her choices. She chose to leave me as a baby in Malawi, and she chose to return to Malawi and leave me with my kids here. It was left to me to make my choices about what I wanted to do with my life. I didn't feel that I owed my mum anything, but I felt I owed my children everything. It has always puzzled me how Malawians visiting England miss home so much that they can't wait to return to Malawi. They complain about the food here (they missed *nsima*, the local food) and they complain about the weather. Me, I have always been happy living here. This is where I grew up. It is my home. I like eating different foods, and although the weather did bother me initially, I learnt to have the appropriate clothing, and to just get on with it.

My family in Malawi would say how very lucky I was, the fact that we had gone to England and got an education. What did I have to complain about? When I tried to say how I felt, they would tell me I was much better off than a lot of people, especially in Malawi. But I didn't see myself as very lucky at all. I kept all my feelings inside. I was scared to let them out because I had learnt it was dangerous to express them. I wouldn't be liked; I would be ostracized – so I kept my feelings to myself, boiling over, like my mum before me and her mother. I had experienced my grandmother's anger only once in my life. I had been playing at the top by the road at our farm in Dowa with one of my mum's cousins, who lived a mile away. It was getting dark, and in Africa it gets dark suddenly. As I walked down the track that led to our house, I heard some rustling in the cornfield, which, at that time of year, was very tall, much taller than me. Anyway, I became scared and called to my friend asking if I could go home with her until an adult could walk me home. (There had been gossip about a man who was snatching little children, and this had been on my mind.) There was no one immediately available to walk me home. Then I was asked to eat with them first, as dinner was ready. I was absolutely bricking it because I knew Grandma would be worried about me, and there were no phones in the villages to call home to let her know I was safe. When an adult was eventually available to walk me home, we walked the back way, not on the main road. My grandmother did not stop shouting when she saw me. She shouted and shouted and shouted, and she did not stop shouting. I just let it go over my head. There was nothing I could have done in the circumstances, and I was secretly pleased because I knew she was shouting because she loved me and thought she had lost me. And she was shouting because she had promised my mum that she would look after me.

Mum had to give up practising midwifery when we children came to live in England. The nearest hospital in Berkshire was in Reading, and she could not yet drive, so she had to take public transport. After a few months of doing this, it became obvious she could not keep it up, what with trying to get enough sleep during the day, plus looking after the three of us. My mum worked at the psychiatric hospital where Dad worked, which was a twenty-minute walk away. In the last years before she retired, she worked at the Mother and Baby Unit attached to the psychiatric hospital, which she enjoyed very much. I remember one summer when my friend Donna and I befriended an American woman who was in the Mother and Baby Unit. We used to hang around there by the river and met her every afternoon. We must have been ten or eleven, but we were shocked when she told us that the father of her baby had abandoned them.

~~~

My dad was a very complex character. To me he seemed domineering and controlling, but he was also very giving. One of my first memories of him when we arrived in England was him and Mum taking us to the cinema in Wantage to see *The Sound of Music*; it was our very first trip to the cinema. When we arrived home, the three of us were buzzing around Mum talking about the film and my dad must have felt left out. So he asked what we were talking about. I turned around to him and snapped, "Mind your own business," a line I had heard in the film. Mum and Dad had to take me aside and explain that what I said was not an appropriate way to speak to an adult. I was such a fiery character, even at that age.

My dad had arrived in Edinburgh with £5 in his pocket. After a year, he had saved up enough money for my mum to come over. They studied to become nurses. By the time we arrived in 1968, they had finished their studies and moved to England. He was working at a psychiatric hospital in Cholsey called Fairmile Hospital. He left home before we were awake and came home after 8pm. He would have an hour with us before we went to bed at 9pm. The job came with accommodation and we lived in a three-bedroomed hospital house, which didn't have any central heating. In the evenings, we would all huddle around a two-bar electric fire, playing cards. I don't think we got a television until 1970; it had BBC1 and ITV, and later my dad had BBC2 installed because he liked to watch operas, classical concerts and programmes like Panorama, much to our disgust. Those were the days before video recorders, so if you didn't watch a programme when it was on, you simply missed it altogether.

This is something I never understood about my dad. Whenever we had guests, and we did often – people from Malawi or from the embassy who were visiting the UK – Dad would go around and ask them what they wanted to drink. Rather than saying to them, "We have this, this and this to drink," if they asked for something we didn't have, he would send one of us to the village shop up the road to buy whatever they had ordered. His behaviour really bugged me, especially when it was me who was sent to the shops.

At that time, I remember that he hit my mum once. They had some sort of argument, I can't remember what about. We were told to go up to our rooms and called down once the row was over. My mum continued to cook dinner and we carried on in silence. When they met, my dad had made her promises to entice her to go out with him. Only once did she mention this. I don't know what he promised her. She never said. She never said it again. She just got on with life. I guess she learnt the hard way the promises men make. She was always very proud though that she worked hard and earned her own money and was not beholden to anyone. It must have been tough for her because back in Malawi, the whole family would have been responsible for raising the children, and she found herself in a foreign country with no back-up.

When I moved to London to live with Alistair, whom I later married, my dad continued to dominate my life. He would ring me, blurt out a whole load of stuff that he expected of me, and before I could reply or put my point of view across, he had hung up. This was the only way that he knew how to have a relationship with me. Each time he hung up, I would say to myself, "Next time I will say something... Next time, next time." Until one day, I did. As soon as I picked up the phone and knew it was him, I blurted out, "What do you want?" He was so shocked that he put the phone down. Later, I heard that he told Mum that I was not to speak to him in that way. What about the way he was speaking to me?

That was the turning point of my relationship with my dad. I remember my younger brother's 21st birthday. He wasn't that bothered and said he didn't want a fuss, but Dad insisted he should have a celebration and rang me up to tell me that we should come. I didn't really want to go because my brother had said he wasn't bothered about it and I was six months pregnant with my daughter. Eventually, we did go and took my sister-in-law's sister, who was staying with us. I overheard my dad talking to her, badmouthing me. I was so shocked and angry; I felt numb that my own dad should do such a thing.

He would also tell us strictly that we were not to swap our Malawi passports for British ones. Well, I eventually decided to get a British passport because I was fed up of taking days off work to go and queue up at embassies to get a visa every time I wanted to travel to another country. I was entitled to a British passport because I had been resident here for a long time and through marriage, and this is what I did. I didn't tell my dad because I knew what his response would be. Anyway, while visiting him and Mum in Malawi with the kids, I was with my dad at the hotel reception when I handed them my passport. It was British, and that was the first time my dad knew about it. He said something like, "You have a British passport, eh?" and I said I did and it was left at that. Soon after, he applied for a British passport.

When he moved to Malawi permanently, he often came back to England and stayed with my brother or friends. The day before he was returning to Malawi, he would contact me and tell me he was leaving the following day. I would be overcome with anxiety because I wanted him to see my children. After a few times of this happening, the next time he came and behaved in this manner, I just wished him a safe journey home and wished him well. He didn't behave like that again, because he knew I wasn't going to put up with it.

A few years before he died, we started to reconcile. He would ring up in plenty of time, so we could make arrangements to see him. One time, while speaking to him on the phone, I asked him why he had kept me at a distance; I had always felt that throughout my relationship with him. His answer was that he did not want to commit incest with me. I wish I had never asked him. What was I to do with that information? On his last trip here, when he knew that his illness could not be cured (he was coming for medical treatment), I was able to thank him for being my dad and for everything he did for me, and tell him that I loved him and that although we had just divorced, Alistair, the kids and I were going to be okay. I was happy with how far I had come with Dad. He wasn't ready to die yet. He wanted extra time. But his maker had other plans for him.

It is common knowledge that my dad fathered children other than the four of us, before Rabson and after Peter, but he did not support them like he supported us. One day, I asked him why. He said that with us, he had wanted to make a go of it, the family thing. In November 1998, just before James started school, I took my children to Malawi to visit my parents. One day this woman came to visit who was much older than me. My mum entertained her, but Dad couldn't wait to get out of the house; he was taking me and my children to the swimming pool. Once at the swimming pool, I asked him who the woman was. He said she was his daughter. He fathered her when he was 14. "Are there any more?" I asked, because this was the second one that I had met. He said there weren't, but this was a lie, because there are others.

My dad was very anti-Malawi when he came to the UK. He was afraid to go back because of the way the Malawi government treated people who had left the country without government permission. Over time, my uncles and other friends enticed him to go back, saying that it was now safe for him to return. In 1975, he returned for the first time and felt very much humbled by the reception he received. He visited many times and started to plan for his retirement there. He always said that it was not a holiday going to Malawi, but he understood that it was his home and that is where he belonged. He also understood that he was nothing without my mum, and he would never let me badmouth her.

My dad had done so many things in his life, crossed so many boundaries. I am very proud of him and everything he achieved and the start he gave us. Looking back now, I can forgive my parents everything, because I now know and understand that everything that happens to us happens for a reason. We choose to be born into a family where we will be shaped by the lessons we learn within that family. And because we are all powerful spiritual beings having a human experience, we have the power to look at everything that happened to us as a lesson we sought to learn in order to fulfil our life purpose.

Dad was mad about Robert Burns, the Scottish poet. During his stay in Scotland, he had come to love Robert Burns and his work, to the extent that even when he left Scotland, he would host his own Burns Nights and he would recite reams and reams of Robert Burns' poetry. I could never understand this infatuation. This summer, I actually spent a couple of weeks in Scotland and visited Robert Burns' birthplace in

Alloway, Ayrshire. Only then did I understand how the young Lucius, coming to Scotland from Malawi, would have become infatuated with Robert Burns and the Scottish people. I was so glad that I was able to connect with my dad in this way.

Letter to my 60-year-old self, 21st July 2020

Dear Maggie,

How are you, and how are you doing? I am writing to you to give you some encouragement.

I know you are feeling a little uncertain about yourself right now and wondering whether you can write this book that you have been wanting to write for so long. I want to tell you that you can do it and have done it. You have everything in your DNA to bring this book to fruition. And what is more important is that it will be your own work, how you have experienced the world – and that is so special, because not many people have the courage and persistence to do that. But I know you have it in abundance. So don't be discouraged; just put your head down and put pen to paper.

The story you are going to tell is within you – you merely need to tell it to the world, and Ellen has agreed to help you. How cool is that? This is your offering and by writing it, you will be helping many people. You will encourage them to tell their story, too. You will get to this day, your 60th birthday, with a lot of love and pride for yourself, and just to let you know that I am so proud of you. I love you more than words can say.

Stop listening to the negative voices in your head, and to people that don't want you to do well. If your family love you, they will want the best for you, whatever makes you happy. They may be resistant at first, but they will come round. Trust me, no one ever stays angry forever – life is too short for that.

I LOVE YOU, MAGGIE.

Go for it!

Reflection

The quote I chose to begin the first chapter was huge, because I was literary risking everything for a dream that no one could understand but me, and at the time I had so many doubts and anxieties about whether I could do it or not. Beginning to write this book was difficult for me, because I was scared of putting my feelings on paper, not just as diary entries, which I had been doing for years, but with a view to other people reading it. It was a very scary experience indeed, and I can't tell you how relieved I was once I had finished writing it. What was also nice was that my mum was happy for me to write it and we started having long conversations about it during lockdown. I must add here that my parents achieved so much while they were in this country. They worked for 30 years in the NHS before retiring back to Malawi. In this chapter, I was merely concentrating on the anger that I had stored up inside around them. Since relinquishing my anger, I have nothing but respect for my parents and everything they did to pave the way for us in this country.

"We come into this world alone, and we go out alone, and for a large part of our lives we are alone with our thoughts. If we are to survive, the answers have to come from within ourselves."

Betty Shine

Chapter 2:
My Brothers

"If you devote your life to achieving your goal, you will not be bothered by shallow criticism. In fact, nothing important can be accomplished if you allow yourself to be swayed by some trifling matter, always looking over your shoulder and wondering what others are saying or thinking. The key to achievements is to move forward resolutely along your chosen path."

Daisaku Ikeda

I was all set to write a chapter on the three women who helped me on my journey, but when I woke up, I had strong emotions, mainly anger about my three brothers. While chanting, I managed to write seven pages in my diary about this anger, so I figured that this week's chapter had chosen itself. This reminded me of a programme I had seen about Alice Walker, who said that before writing a book, she would invite her characters to come and live in her house with her, and they would go on their journey together. Only in my case, the characters are inviting themselves.

I have three brothers: two older than me and one younger, who was born in the UK in 1970 after we had been here for two years. My eldest brother informs me that Grandad died in July 1969, and a year later, in July 1970, Mum gave birth to Peter.

I was always with my two brothers. I followed them everywhere. I guess I had the closest relationship with my middle brother Paul, because there is only a year between us. I remember my first day at school in Malawi; Paul held my hand. And when we came to live in England, I didn't mind because I had my two brothers to protect me. But it was Paul who started crying when our parents were driving us from the airport to our new home in Cholsey, which was then in Berkshire. I remember Dad had to stop the car in a lay-by near Henley while Mum comforted Paul, saying that everything would be alright.

When we started at the local village school, we were put in the bottom class, and we sat next to each other. Although in Malawi we had attended a European school as soon as we knew we were coming to England, our English language was not yet quite up to scratch.

I think Paul and I were very lucky to have some years at primary school, because it was such fun. During secondary school, Paul became more distant. He hung out with his friends and he didn't want his little sister following him around, although that is what I would have rather been doing because some of his friends were gorgeous. He also loved football; he first supported Everton, then Arsenal, and spent weekends travelling to London to see matches.

He and his friends would try and travel to London and back on the train without paying by hiding in the toilets when the inspector came around. One time he got caught and was detained by the police. The police rang my dad to tell him what Paul had done. Dad was so angry, he told the police to keep him locked up. Mum, who was at his side, pleaded with Dad to get him out, which he did. Another time, Paul found himself stranded at Didcot after a night out in London, and he phoned Dad in the early hours to come and get him. Dad refused, and Paul ended up walking home all by himself, which was about five miles. I always felt this was such different behaviour from my friend Susan's dad, who always told Susan that it didn't matter what time she rang him, he would come out and get her.

While growing up, I was never allowed out as much as the boys, and I remember I would be dying for Paul to come home and tell me everything that had happened at this party or dance, who was there, who danced with who, who got off with who, all that sort of stuff. He wouldn't tell me immediately, but in his own time, when he was ready. This could take days, weeks or months, but he would tell me everything I wanted to know and more about what happened at the dance or party he had gone to. He had observed it all. He was my ears and eyes.

He left home the same time I left home. I got married and other things occupied my mind. My underlying experience of my brother was him trying to boss me about and me resisting. That is still the case to this day.

We had a falling out more than 10 years ago. My kids were in secondary school and his daughter was two. He had brought her to stay with us for the weekend. He and her mother were no longer together. The relationship had broken down around the time their daughter was born. He told me he had found another woman in Malawi, and he asked me not to tell the old girlfriend, as I did speak to her from time to time. I couldn't believe what I was hearing, because I felt he was putting me in a very awkward position. I told him he should tell his old girlfriend himself that he had a new partner. When I told him this, he was so mad. He called me all these names I will not repeat. It was about 1am and he had just come back from the pub with Alistair (my husband at the time). He picked his daughter up from where she was sleeping, put her in the car and drove home all the way to Swindon. He refused to talk to me. Whenever I tried to call him, he wouldn't speak to me because he was so angry with me for not supporting him.

It is a cultural thing for men to misbehave and for women to look the other way, but I didn't like this. My grandmother, who would have been the person to put a stop to this sort of behaviour, actually encouraged it and she would entertain her other sons' families at her home. When one of my aunts confronted her about this, she replied that she used to run to the bottom of the garden when her husband was beating her boys, and this for her was compensating for not having protected them from him. My mother continued my grandmother's habit of looking the other way. I wouldn't have been able to stand up to my brother had I not been in therapy. I am so grateful that I was. I had no intention of looking the other way. He was wrong to suspect that I would. We were far removed from our culture, so we could do better.

Paul didn't speak to us for three or four years after that incident, but then he invited us to his 50th birthday party. I felt this was a major breakthrough. By this time, my husband and I were no longer together and I had moved to a smaller house in Nunhead. I went with the kids to the party. My ex went with his new partner. It was the early days of the split, but we were all making the best of a difficult situation. The invitation to Paul's birthday party signified the end of the rift, but things were never really the same.

The following year, our dad died. Paul had fallen out with him because he had felt that Dad was using him and his flat when he came to the UK on his visits. They had had words, and split. On my 49th birthday, which was after we had moved to the new house, I had a birthday/housewarming party and invited Dad, who was in the country. I also invited Paul because I thought it would be a good opportunity for them to meet. Dad really wanted to see Paul. He kept asking me about him, and he wanted to see if he had any mail for him. But Paul didn't show up. I knew this would be the last time I would see him and by November, Dad had passed away. I was so angry at Paul about that.

Last year was 10 years since Dad died, and Paul was angry with me and shouted at me because I said I couldn't afford to go to Malawi for the anniversary. At the same time, he shouted at me for being in debt and unable to afford to go to Malawi for the unveiling of my daughter Lonie's tombstone. He said: "You must go. It can't go ahead without you." This just pushed me into depression. I had worked hard to go to Malawi. I had been for Lonie's funeral. I had been for Mum's 80th birthday, and I had been for Paul's 60th. Paul had wanted a big party in Malawi for his 60th birthday and he invited many family and friends. None of his friends came from England because of the cost. I found it all very stressful.

We were busy organising the party when we heard that our

Aunt Deria in Lilongwe, who had been very ill, had passed away the Wednesday before. The party was scheduled for Saturday. My aunt had looked after us when we were awaiting clearance from the government in 1968 and of course I felt I had to go to the funeral. So we went to Lilongwe for the funeral (a 500-mile trip) and we were arriving back really late Friday evening to get Paul's party going the next day. I was just thinking, *This is not how I want my 60th birthday to be. I would like space to reflect on my life, not all this stress.* A few days before the party, we had gone to Dad's village and invited family there, but this proved to be a disaster. They came, but instead of enjoying the party, a minority of them were stealing bottles of beer, putting them in their bags, and taking the meat that was meant for the barbecue. Mum said she had warned Paul about this, and that is why Dad never invited any of his family anywhere because he knew they would misbehave. I was angry with Paul at his party when in his speech, he told everyone that he was coming back to live in Malawi, and so were Peter and me. I was so mad because he hadn't discussed it with me, and I didn't know what I wanted. I would like to think that I will make that decision myself when the time comes.

I remember a year before, Paul and I had travelled to Malawi for Mum's 80th birthday. The following morning Paul was driving me to the tailor's to have our outfits made for the party, because we all needed to wear the same cloth. On the way he had road rage, shouting about the stupid driving in the country. I couldn't believe it. We had just arrived in the country, and he was not grateful to be here, just angry. I was so shocked I just kept my mouth shut. When we arrived at the shop, there were two tailors either side. He went to one to explain how he wanted his outfit sewn; I went to the other. When he had finished explaining, he came over to me and started to butt into the conversation between me and my tailor. I turned around to him and said, "Just shut up," because I couldn't think with him there. He wasn't pleased, but he backed off.

When we were walking back to the car, still angry, he said to me, "Don't you ever talk to me like that again."

I replied: "And don't you ever talk to me like that." I don't know where that came from, but I felt great.

We drove in silence to Blantyre, where he dropped me off. He was very angry, but I don't know why. He didn't explain why he was so angry. But I know I don't want to spend the rest of my life angry, or in the company of people who are angry. I have worked too hard for that. Paul hasn't had the responsibility of bringing up kids full-time. He has had his daughter for a few days a week here and there. Anyone can do that.

Paul and Peter don't really get on. There is a lot of tension there. Paul gets angry just at the mention of Peter's name. Maybe because he can't boss him around, because Peter went to live in Germany and cut himself off from the family. When I asked Peter about it in a conversation recently, he said it was because of the 11-year age gap. He felt they didn't really have a lot in common.

I was also angry at Paul for bossing me around about going to Malawi for the tenth anniversary of our dad's passing last November and Lonie's tombstone unveiling when I was not in the right space financially, emotionally or physically. He never really had much time for Lonie anyway. She was always trying to get in touch with him. She loved her uncle and cousin, but he never seemed to have much time for her. For Lonie, family was everything. I felt her pain whenever she talked about her uncles and how she never saw them. I would tell her one day we would; it would be alright in the end. She never got to meet her German cousins. Lonie's birthday comes and goes, and I don't hear a word from him.

The anniversary of her death, I hear nothing from him. But he won't stop harping on about her tombstone unveiling. It doesn't make much sense to me. I don't feel I had to be at her tombstone unveiling. I would remember her in my way. Also, as a Buddhist, I believe that the person's soul lives on and is with us throughout eternity.

I sent Paul a letter. "Why didn't you see Dad when he came on his last visit? He wanted to see you. He was asking me if you had any mail for him. It was heart-breaking for me to see him like that. I guess he wanted to see you for the last time to say goodbye, but you wouldn't see him. Why? It would have been a chance for you to say goodbye to him. I had to take the brunt of that. I didn't know why you didn't want to see him. You were angry. He was an old man, and dying. He was asking to see you. And now you are the one who is telling me I must go to Malawi to commemorate 10 years since he died. What is that all about? I was there for him when he asked me to be. I drove up to Maidstone to see him. I drove him to see the priest because he didn't want to die yet. He wanted to ask for extra time. He thought seeing a priest here in England would do the trick.

"And Lonie always wanted to see you, but you had no time for her when she was alive. You were too busy. Now that she is dead you are busy saying I should do this, I should do that, like attend her tombstone unveiling. I am telling you I can't go because I can't afford it, because I have been three times already for her funeral, for Mum's 80th birthday and for your 60th birthday. Now I find myself overdrawn, when I don't have a job. I had worked hard to go to Malawi last year, and I hated it when I was there. I found it very stressful. The funeral, your party – it was stressful. I was shattered when I got back. I went into lockdown last August. I fell into depression because I was tired and I didn't know what to do next. I didn't know where my life was heading. I didn't feel in control. I kept away from all of you because I couldn't cope. I didn't contact you, Mum, Peter or Rabs for six months because of the way I was feeling. And I noticed that none of you contacted me either..."

~~~

My youngest brother Peter (he also likes to be called Lucius, our dad's name) was born in the UK in July 1970, so he has a different experience to my two elder brothers and me. When

Mum was pregnant with him, I wanted him to be a girl because I wanted to have a friend. When he came along, I fell in love with him immediately. We children were not allowed to visit him in hospital in Wallingford, but when he came home and Dad put him in my arms, it was love at first sight. I was given a lot of responsibility for my little brother. Most of the time I was alright about it. But there were times when I would rather be doing something with my friends, and then I did mind.

When Peter left school he stayed around Oxford for a while, working in fashion shops, and then he met his long-term girlfriend Denise, who is German, and moved to Dusseldorf to live. He cut himself off from the family. He has four children – two boys and two girls – who we have never met.

We started talking on Facebook here and there, and recently on WhatsApp, and I have spoken to him on the telephone twice. He has been really interested in me writing this book and has been quick to air his grievances about his childhood. He has many questions for me about when he was growing up because he can't remember as he was too young. I have been happy to fill him in.

When I asked him if we could come and visit when his first child was born, he was so angry, he shouted at me down the phone. His anger was palpable; I don't know what that was about. It seems that is the way my family express themselves. Shout the person down so they can't come back and ask another question. It would frighten the living daylights out of me and I became a scared animal, without a voice, afraid to speak. I don't know why Peter was so angry; he didn't tell me. Lonie had been desperate to meet her German cousins. Lonie was in touch with Denise, but she said it had to be a secret, because Peter would have a fit if he found out. Denise used to send her photos of her cousins.

Before writing this chapter, I was able to write to Peter and express all the anger I felt for him. "I didn't understand why we couldn't meet your family. I didn't understand what was wrong with us. Why were you so angry? I remember you shouting down the phone at me when I suggested that we come to Germany to visit when your first son was born. What was that all about? If you could tell me why you were so angry with me, then I could say sorry. I think it's because you think I didn't like looking after you when you were little. I had too much responsibility for you, and I was just a child myself. I remember you couldn't believe it when I chose to look after my children full-time. They were my children, my responsibility."

When my son was visiting Germany, quite near Peter in Dusseldorf, I asked my brother if he could visit and he bluntly said no. I was very hurt and didn't understand why he would refuse to see my son. I have always felt that I have to be careful what I say to him in case he blocks me on Facebook, which is what used to happen. Lonie and I used to joke about it: "Be careful what you say or he will block you." I don't understand why I am not allowed to see my nephews and nieces.

In our conversation, Peter asked me why I keep going back to Malawi, why I keep going back and scratching at the scabs. Why do I not leave well alone? To this I replied, "The answer is I don't know. I think it has a lot to do with the fact that I don't want to upset anyone and I don't want to be ostracised, cut off from my family. I think I care too much about this, and it is killing me." Can I live in the UK once Paul leaves? I think about it a lot, but I don't know the answers. That is why I am writing this book. To bring clarity to my life. To discover me, where I go from here. What would I do in Malawi? I can't even speak the language and I don't understand the mentality of the people there. Dad often said that he couldn't stay there full time. He had to leave from time to time to keep sane.

Reflection

I have learnt that family are with us throughout our lifetime, so we have to find a way of getting on with them – unlike friends, whom you can ditch when they no longer serve a purpose in your life. I have learnt that it is important to put time aside to be with your family. I had all this anger going on about my brothers that I was not able to express. I am happy now that I have expressed my feelings towards them, and I am now able to have the relationship that I want to have with them without any fear. I am grateful for my brothers because they have helped to shape the person that I have become. The relationship with my brothers is unfinished, I know, but that is because we are all very much alive and are still directing our lives on this stage called life. For me, I know I have put myself in a much better position to direct A 'happy ever after' sort of movie with everything that I now know.

"You can do anything. It doesn't matter what you have done or where you are from,
but you have to take the first step."

Carousel

Chapter 3:
A Tribute to My Eldest Brother

"It's never too late to have a happy childhood."

Tom Robbins

My eldest brother Rabson (we call him Rabs) has announced his retirement at the end of this month (August 2020), so it is fitting that I am writing about him this week. He was born 63 years ago, on 27th July 1957, in Lilongwe Top Hospital and the family moved to Mchinji shortly afterwards, where Mum and Dad were working as nurses. As per custom, word was sent to the grandparents for a name for the newborn, and in the meantime, he was called 'Lad'. They waited and waited, but the name never came. Word has it that Grandad was unhappy about the union because he had wanted Mum to marry into another family, but Dad had come along and swept her off her feet. Eventually, Dad named him Rabson, but the name 'Lad' stuck, and we were calling him Lad well into his teens, Paul and I. Rabson says he was very close to Grandad and they would often have chats, so it seems Grandad did not stay angry for long. Mum described the young Rabson as a cheeky little monkey because he was always getting into trouble.

Those were his carefree days before Paul came along in July 1959, then me in July 1960. Rabson has been around all my life and it feels a little weird trying to put distance between the two of us so I can write about his character, but I will do my best. The three of us attended Kokri School in Lilongwe, and in 1967, when we knew we were going to England, our parents sent us to The European School, also in Lilongwe. We travelled to England together, the three of us, leaving behind all our family and friends and everything we had ever known in Malawi. It was Rabson who took charge of us until we met up with our parents at Heathrow Airport, escorted by an air hostess. He remembers more about this time than I do, being a bit older.

His role as big brother continued once we arrived in this country. Even more so, he became the parent. Dad worked days and Mum worked nights. There was a half-hour gap between Mum leaving for work at 7.30pm and Dad arriving home soon after 8pm. During that time Rabson was in charge, and Paul and I had to do what he said. Paul and I walked to the village school and back with our friends. Rabson, being eleven when we arrived, had a much tougher time as he went straight to secondary school.

I remember once after school I had gone with some friends to a new clothes shop that had opened up in the village. A boy I was trying to impress and I stole a pink shirt. The police traced the boy to his home and he dobbed me in. The police came and knocked on our door during that half-hour that we were home alone. I admitted to the theft, and they gave me a warning and told me never to do it again. I was so lucky with the timing, because God only knows what would have happened to me had either parent been at home at the time. The three of us kept this incident to ourselves and we never mentioned it again. It seemed the fear of what could have happened was in all of us. Rabson took responsibility. That is how we carried on. The three of us against the world.

When Rabson started at secondary school he was the only black boy there initially. Secondary school is tough enough because you move from a small primary school where you know everyone and everyone knows you to a great big school with so many kids that you feel engulfed. Rabson went from Malawi into such a school environment, and he was disadvantaged because English was a second language to him. In order that we could get on in school, Dad banned us from speaking Chichewa at home (which was not one of his best moves, might I add.) But the young Rabson worked very hard at school. Despite his disadvantages, he put his head down and focused on the matter at hand – his schooling. I remember by the time I arrived at secondary school, he was a prefect and not someone you should mess with because he was in a position of authority and could give you detention if you were out of line. As Rabson was in Shackleton House, the best house, Paul and I automatically followed him there. The other houses were Newton, Faraday and Tennyson. Any house points you were given for good work or good behaviour went towards your house and the house with the most points at the end of the year received a cup, so there was a big incentive to do well. I remember a lot of house points were given out on sports day. No one messed with me at secondary school because I had two big brothers to defend me. Rabson excelled and, when he left at sixteen, was awarded with a special prize for being so hard-working. I remember all the family were invited to the evening award ceremony. It was quite an event.

I remember Rabson having a lot of responsibility for Paul and me and, later for Peter when he came along on 14th July 1970 (yet another July birthday). He was very strict and kept the three of us in line. Whenever our parents were away, he was the boss, and we had to do whatever he said. Paul and I wanted to throw parties, but he would say no. Saying that, he did occasionally let us. He was also our parent in that whenever we were in trouble or wanted money, it was him we would go to, as when he started work as a builder's apprentice he always had money. He worked his way up the trade.

In the summer of 1974, Mum took Peter to Malawi for his first visit. I remember Dad booked the three of us in a hotel in Blackpool for two weeks as he was busy with work. Again, Rabson was in charge. We spent most of that holiday not on the beach but in the games room, playing with the other kids (who, like us, had been sent for the summer), arguing about what we were going to watch on the television and fighting over the sofa, so Rabson recalls. He also remembers that it was full board and that an older woman took us to a disco one evening.

When Rabson was 14, Dad managed to secure a job for him as a porter at the hospital where he worked, after school and in the summer holidays. The job involved cleaning the offices, working on the wards serving meals, washing up with the dishwasher and packing the dishes away ready for next time. As a perk of the job, he was allowed to frequent the staff social club where he would play snooker. He also became a member of the football and cricket clubs and he had use of the tennis courts. Rabson was football mad, as were Paul and Peter. He spent a lot of his spare time playing football, or travelling to London to see his favourite team Chelsea play. Peter Osgood was his favourite player, as I remember. His football career spanned the whole time he was in this country. He played for Cholsey Bluebirds, Fairmile Football Team, Benson Football Club, Wallingford United and Didcot Town Football Club, where he played until he left. He won trophies with Benson and Wallingford. Those were the days before black footballers had entered the arena. He remembers this time fondly. His job was well paid, so he was able to fund himself, go out with his friends and save some money.

When he left school, he did a three-year apprenticeship with Boshers, a builder's merchants. He had to attend college in Reading as part of the course. When we moved to Benson, he was able to drive there in his Ford Popular, of which he was very proud; he kept it spotless. No one was allowed to smoke or eat in it. It seemed to me we could hardly breathe when we were in it. When I passed my driving test, he would allow me to borrow it for evenings out with my friends, as long as it was as clean as when I took it, and I had to put in £3 petrol for my usage. His first car had been an Austin Morris, which Dad had bought him as soon as he passed his driving test at age seventeen. He also had a van that he used for work. During the day, he worked in Abingdon. He would come home, get out of his dirty clothes, have a bath, put on clean clothes, then drive to Reading for his evening classes, arriving home at 9pm. He learnt general fitting, painting and carpentry. He also learnt management towards becoming a foreman. Then he went on to learn bricklaying. He worked for Wimpey in Basingstoke, Wokingham and London. Later, he joined David Jones, a family contractor in Ewelme. Here he was able to put his learning into practice, doing painting, carpentry, building and plumbing. I remember him coming home really, really dirty and having to have a bath. He used to have huge cooked breakfasts every morning. Mum and Dad would go to Reading shopping at an Indian shop once a month and bulk buy. They would buy whole chickens, which we would pluck ourselves, then freeze. All the giblets would be left for Rabson's breakfasts.

My dad bought me a lovely Roberts radio, which I was very proud of. Rabson asked if he could take it to work as his was broken. Well, after months on a building site it was wrecked, and I was devastated and felt powerless to do anything about it.

Rabson felt frustrated because he wanted to invest money in some land. He had found some land in Pangbourne, but he kept hitting a brick wall with the purchase when he said he was a foreigner. So, at the age of 25, he decided to go back to Malawi and see what his chances were over there. He left in August 1982. He had to relearn Chichewa, but as he lived with one of our uncles for six months, who had three very chatty children, it didn't take him long to relearn his mother tongue. By January 1983, he had secured a job with Press Properties, one of the big building companies in Malawi, as an assistant works manager. He was later promoted to works manager. When he got married to his wife Anna in August 1988, at the age of 31, the general manager put him in a townhouse as a sitting tenant. They later decided to buy this house. Rabson's first son Sandram was born in 1989, and Kelvin followed in 1992. He educated them and has seen them both married to their respective partners over the last few years.

At Paul's 60th birthday last year, Rabson, in his speech, said, "We used to be close," to which I shouted, "We still are." It was wishful thinking on my part. That closeness we had as children will always be there. It will never leave us. But these days we all have our own lives. Rabson has lived in Malawi now for over thirty years. Paul and I live in the UK – I in London, Paul in Swindon, and his daughter, Makana, in Reading – and Peter lives in Germany with his partner Denise and their four children Noel, Noah, Vivien and Helena (Nella.)

When I look back, I can't help but wonder what life would have been like had Rabson stayed in England, because him leaving as he did at 25 to go to Malawi was rather a wrench for me at the time, because he had been such an important part of my life. I admire him greatly for everything he has achieved and I am also in awe of him because he created his life in such a way that he was always there for the important events. The only funeral he did not attend was Grandad's. He has been there for the others. The other three of us are abroad, living our lives. I was also in awe of Rabson because he has built things. He has something visual to show for his life. While driving around the city of Blantyre, he will point out that he built those offices or that supermarket. His portfolio is most impressive. In comparison, I felt I had nothing to show for my life. Just dreams in my head, which I was too embarrassed to talk about for fear of being laughed at or being told that I was mad. So writing this book has been quite profound for me. I guess being the eldest he had something to prove to the world and himself. Because of him, me being third born gave me the freedom to follow my dream. When I asked him if he was proud of what he has achieved, he said, "I am very proud of what I have achieved. I have worked very hard, brought up my children and educated them, and now they are both married and living their own lives. It is my time now to do what I want to do." I also asked him if he suffered racism as the first black boy in his secondary school. He said he hadn't. It was more that people were interested in him. They wanted to touch his hair. They were very open with him and he felt welcomed wherever he went, as he travelled around a lot playing football.

Reflection

I often wonder what would have happened had my brother stayed in the UK. How different would our relationship have been? But he felt obliged to go back to Malawi and build a life for himself there. Being so far away, I do not see him often, so when I do see him, I make the most of each moment I am with him. I do get annoyed that he doesn't take any time off when I visit so we can go on a trip or something, but now that he has retired, that will no longer be a problem. While writing this book and talking to my brother about his life, I wondered where I was while he was getting his education because we were living in the same house. It just goes to show that we were living parallel lives, each following his or her dream, what we believed our life purpose to be. I realise now that I was right to follow my dream, even though it was not as tangible as my brother's. By following my dream, I have become happy. I can only imagine that Rabson also followed his dream and it has made him happy, too.

"I grew up with an older brother, and the bond between siblings is unlike anything else, and it can be a real journey to accept what that bond is once you both mature into it. Because it's not always what you want. It's not always what you expect. It's not always what you imagined or hoped. But it's one of the most important things in the world."

Ben Schnetzer

Chapter 4:
Marriage

"People come into our lives for a reason, a season or a lifetime. Some will bring lessons, blessings, and some will be both. Many will leave a profound impact on your journey, some good, some indifferent, and some will bring you trauma. Regardless, they will bring or be a player in an experience you need to further your evolution. Some we will welcome with love, some leave us with a familiar feeling of 'What just happened?' and will actually be a part of our journey long term, and some will become our closest friend and confidant. Nonetheless, when their part on our journey is over, we need to thank them even for the pain they brought with our love. They came into our lives at precisely the right moment and brought the exact experience we needed at that time. Let go of the attachments you had with them, allow yourself to learn, heal and grow from the shared experience and quietly move on, always, and in all ways, with love.

Unknown

I met Alistair at the African Centre in Covent Garden on 2nd April 1982, the day after April Fool's Day. My Uncle Patrick was working at the High Commission in London and would invite my brothers and me to parties in London. This particular time, my friend Susan was also with us. It was a party for Malawian students and Alistair was there because he had just returned from a two-year stay in Malawi, working at the statistics office in Zomba, so he had Malawian friends who had invited him. Alistair was talking to my brother Paul when I went up and interrupted their conversation to tell my brother something. I realised what I had done, turned around to Alistair, apologised to him and offered him a garlic sweet (I had these left over from April Fool's Day.) I bumped into him later and asked him if he had liked his sweet. He said it didn't go with his beer. We ended up dancing together and, later, snogging. He asked me for my address, so he could come to Oxford to see me, but I refused to give it to him. He said if I didn't give it to him, he would ring the embassy and get it from my uncle. I said I wouldn't want him to go to all that trouble, so I gave it to him.

I received a letter from him three weeks later. He said he had been trying to arrange accommodation at one of the Oxford colleges through a friend that had gone there. The weekend he came to visit me, I was still living at my parents' home in Benson, but my friend Susan and I were seeing Cliff Richard at a theatre in Oxford on the Friday evening, so we arranged to meet Alistair in the pub opposite. After the show I had second thoughts, and asked Susan if we could sneak out and go to another bar. But Alistair had anticipated that we might do that and made sure he was at the front door waiting for us. I asked Susan to come into the pub with us until I felt comfortable about being left with this stranger I hardly knew. She left after one drink. That night I went back to Benson, to my parents' house, but I came back into Oxford the next day, having borrowed my brother's car. Alistair and I drove to Blenheim Palace, a favourite place of mine I had first visited on a primary school trip. We spent the day there in the grounds; we didn't go into the house as we were rather besotted with each other. That evening we had our first dinner together at Browns. I remember Alistair said, "This is the turning point of our relationship. Who is going to pay the bill?" The bill was £5. I wasn't going to squabble about that. I was happy for him to pay the bill; that was what I was used to. I also drove back to Oxford to spend the day with him on Sunday. It was a perfect weekend. I was about to move into my own bedsit on the Abingdon Road and this would make it easier for us to see each other.

Once I was settled in my bedsit, Alistair would come and stay every other weekend; sometimes he would bring his bike on the train so we could go cycling. One day, we cycled to Benson on the back roads, and Alistair met my parents, who we found in their allotment. We also loved going to the cinema. Oxford, being a university city, had plenty of cinema houses that showed independent films. We shopped for food, we cooked, we met up with my friends, mostly. While Alistair had lived in Malawi, he had found it difficult to get to know or date Malawian girls, as in Malawi, as soon as you are seen with a girl, people assume you are practically married. He couldn't believe his luck when he met me. I was Malawian, but also English, and he liked my family very much. I think he liked my family too much actually, looking back. He felt that he had a lot to teach me (academically), and I felt that I had a lot to teach him too (generally). I was never intimidated by him. Money was always a big contention between us, because from the very start, Alistair had more money than me. I remember once I said to him that I didn't want to come to London one particular weekend, because I wanted to buy a new dress, and I couldn't afford to do both. This did not go down well with him, and from then on, he agreed to subsidise me.

After eighteen months of going back and forth between London and Oxford, we decided this coming and going was too much for us, and that I should move to London. I managed to get a transfer to Barclays Bank in Bond Street. Alistair's parents had helped him to put down a deposit on a flat and that's where we lived. First Alistair was working at the Treasury, then he started doing a PhD at the London School of Economics. I found it difficult to make my own friends in London, as most of us working at the bank lived too far out of the city, so my social life consisted of Alistair's friends, and initially I enjoyed it. They were mainly from Cambridge University, where Alistair had gone.

Alistair's mum and sister were not too pleased about our

union. His sister said it wouldn't last because we were so different, and his mum, who was Jewish, said, "It's not because you're black, dear; it's because you're uneducated." She meant because I hadn't been to university, and she would prefer that he marry a nice Jewish girl. Once when his parents came to visit us at the flat, Alistair and his dad went to The Clock House pub nearby, and his mum and I stayed at the flat. She basically told me she wanted me to move out of the flat because I wasn't suitable for Alistair. I held my ground. When Alistair and his dad returned, they found us exactly where they had left us – in deadlock, neither of us giving way. His mum died the following year, in 1985. She'd had breast cancer 10 years previously which came back and took her.

The year after, on 2nd August 1986, and four years after we met, Alistair and I were married in Benson. We also went to Malawi and had a wedding in my mum's village and another in my dad's. You could say we were wedded out. Then we went to Victoria Falls in Zambia for our honeymoon before coming back to England and settling into married life. By this time, I was working as a receptionist in an estate agent's nearby, having left the bank and worked as a temp. Later, I enrolled at Goldsmiths College to do a social science degree. I was still trying to navigate my way to what I wanted to do.

Within a year of being married, we had enrolled for marriage counselling with Relate, as we were having problems. I felt that I had lost myself. I used to dread going to see my husband's family. It used to take me two weeks to work up to it, and two weeks to recover from it. I dreaded spending Christmas at his parents' house and, equally, I dreaded spending it at my parents', so we decided to spend Christmas on our own, but see the family around the holidays. That seemed to work much better. Looking back, I feel I was a buffer for my husband between him and his family. I was the one who was showing all the emotions. I remember being referred to as 'being too emotional', whatever that means.

By the time I graduated from university, I was eight

months pregnant with our daughter. Lonie came along on 22nd October 1991 and changed our lives forever. I had a C-section and spent seven days in hospital. My mum came to help out. Our second child James was born on 16th June 1994. This time my mum did not come. I had now started therapy and things had become quite tense between us, as I had started to unravel my life in the sessions. Mum had received news that one of her brothers in Malawi was ill, and she chose to go there instead of coming to be with me while I had my son. There seemed to be a pattern to her behaviour. We managed without her. Lonie went to stay with a neighbour and Alistair split himself between the hospital and Lonie. My mum came to visit on her return from Malawi, but I had long lost caring.

I remember Lonie did not want to be sent away to nursery when James was born. She wanted to stay home and help care for her brother. It was another six months before she agreed to go. They were great friends. She was very into family; she wanted to know all her family, here and in Malawi, and she just wanted everyone to get on. James was a bundle of joy and was into everything. I knew from the start that he was destined for the world, so I made sure that I enjoyed every moment of those eighteen years that he lived at home.

I stayed home to look after the children, something I wanted to do because I had missed that time with my mum. They both went to the local church school, St John's and St Clements in East Dulwich, and then later to The Charter School in North Dulwich. When they were in school, I read my therapy books, attended therapy, went to yoga classes and took various courses, one of which was a post-graduate diploma in counselling at Goldsmiths College; I had a placement at Mind in Purley. But Alistair and I grew further and further apart. We were hankering after different things, and there never seemed to be time to sit down and talk about the future, or anything, really.

We had moved house to be in the catchment area of the children's school. This had been my decision, as it meant the children would not have to travel far to school. Soon after our move, Alistair started to work abroad in Finland for weeks at a time, and I was left to mind the children alone. We visited him in the holidays. One summer, when we were visiting Lapland, the two of us went out for a meal to celebrate our 20th wedding anniversary. That's when he told me he didn't want to be married to me anymore, and he chucked his wedding ring away, saying it had never been his decision to move house. I was shocked. I didn't believe it. I thought he had lost all his senses. I knew things were not perfect, and I was in therapy unravelling my part, and I thought everything would be alright in the end. But I guess it was not enough for one person to try to make it work. We both needed to be in therapy, working towards the same goal. I travelled back to the UK with the kids, still in shock, but I was confident that he would change his mind – until I learnt from friends that he was living with someone in Finland. I confronted him with this, and said he couldn't come back to the house. That's when he became very angry. I was trying to process it all and what this would mean for me and the children. He wanted me to move out of the family home, sell it and downsize.

Eventually, on 24th April 2009, the kids and I moved to a smaller house in Nunhead. I managed to get a part-time job as a receptionist on the labour ward at King's College Hospital and gave up my counselling placement at Mind. My supervisor said I needed time out to 'lick my wounds'. Alistair was paying me alimony and paying for the kids until they were 18. I had a solicitor, Vivien Piercy, who was brilliant, and my therapist Juliet was also helping me. On the court day, I also had a brilliant barrister working for me, who asked for a very good package for me, so in that regard I was happy.

Alistair and his girlfriend moved to the UK with her son. Lonie wanted to live with him, as she was a daddy's girl, but he refused. It was a very difficult time.

I was there for the kids as much as I could be at the time. Alistair's girlfriend's son was in the same school as my kids;

that was difficult for me. Alistair was really pressing my buttons. Lonie wanted us to talk, because she needed support from the both of us, but Alistair would not talk to me. He was so angry. I couldn't understand why he was angry. He had wanted a divorce, and now he had it, but he remained angry, unable to communicate with me even for the good of our children. Initially he lived nearby, but I was relieved when he moved out of London, as it meant that I wouldn't bump into him or his girlfriend, who he married as soon as the divorce was settled. I must add here that Vivien Piercy, the solicitor who helped me with the divorce, had been recommended to me by a woman I had befriended on my street. It turned out that this woman (whose name I cannot remember) was also from Benson, the village I grew up in, and had babysat for Juliet, my therapist. It just goes to show that it is such a small world.

Reflection

Alistair came into my life for a season of my life, at precisely the right time, and brought the exact experience that I needed in order to further my evolution. I am grateful to him for the experience and revisiting this very painful period in my life has helped me tremendously to let go of the hurt and trauma I experienced. I am very grateful for the 25 years we had together. We had two beautiful children who I raised myself. In the divorce settlement I had a house and the kids. He pays me alimony, so I don't have to worry about bills and food. I have a lodger and a part-time job as a nanny, and I have been able to pursue the things that make me happy – my yoga and my healing work and writing this book. I am grateful for everything that happened and for the lessons I learned along the way.

"A broken heart is a heart that will not let the lover go, that calls love possession and not expression. The mind must be trained to stay in the present so that when a lover leaves you, you are still present and accept the verdict – with tears, yes, but not the years of suffering the untrained mind inflicts on the poor human involved. The suffering of a broken heart is a self-inflicted gunshot that is being repeated over and over, day by day, minute by minute. This is not the lover's doing, but yours – by staying in the place of judgment and lack of acceptance. Let us make sure we are truthful in this story we are telling ourselves. Did we perhaps betray ourselves and refuse to acknowledge this? Did we perhaps not see the signs and blame the other for our lack of attention? All these things must be looked at to heal past hurts and truly let them go so that your heart can be open for the experience of a new and exciting love that will lead you to heaven, hand in hand with the one you offer your heart to."

Tina Louise Spalding

Chapter 5:
My Three Mentors

"When the student is ready, the teacher will appear."

Tao Te Ching

Juliet

I was about 20 when I met the woman who would become my first mentor. At this time I was working in Oxford as a secretary at Barclays Bank. It was okay for a first job, but I knew this was not where I was destined to spend my years. We were situated in Carfax on the first floor, overlooking Cornmarket Street and the High Street. I remember looking down at the streets, which were packed with tourists from all over the world in the summer months, thinking, "What are all these people doing milling around outside? Haven't they got jobs to go to? And how come I am stuck here all day long? Why am I not down there milling around with everyone else?" It just seemed more fun than where I was, answering the phone all day long, connecting people to different departments, typing letters to people telling them how much they were overdrawn by and if they didn't pay it by a certain date, they would be fined, etc. Being truthful, it was boring, but I tried not to think about it too much. I was earning money and I had my independence. What more could a girl my age want? I knew I wasn't staying at the bank, so I never took out any loans for cars or mortgages like a lot of my colleagues.

One day I came out of the bank just in time to catch the Reading 5 bus, which would take me home. The journey took an hour as the bus stopped at every village along the way. At the stop I spotted a tall blonde girl around my age. She was stunning, but she also caught my eye because she had a four-year-old boy with her, and they were wearing the same jumpers. I sat upstairs at the front of the bus and they came upstairs too and sat somewhere behind me. From time to time I looked back to see them playing together; the rest of the time I chilled after my long day. They got off the bus in the same village as me, Benson, and that's when we spoke. I asked her if the little boy was hers and she said no, she was an au pair from Norway and she was living in the village with his family. Her name was Heidi and the little boy's name was Julian.

From that day on, we started meeting up and going out. Someone said we looked like misfits walking down the street together, her tall and blonde and me being black, I guess. We gravitated towards one another because we were different and didn't belong. The little boy Julian had a very good friend called Joe, who lived opposite them. I was with Heidi when she went to pick Julian up from Joe's house and that's when I met Joe's mum, Juliet. I had no idea at the time that she was going to play such an important part in my journey towards enlightenment. Had I known, maybe I would have run a mile. The Universe only gives us what we need to know today. Juliet was brown and from Guyana, and she was in a mixed marriage. This would be why I would gravitate towards her in later years.

After that first meeting, I met Juliet again at a party Heidi's family had, and she encouraged me to come and see her whenever I wanted, which I did. I always enjoyed her company, and I babysat for her four children a few times. She was training to be a yoga teacher, and she invited me to attend her trainee classes, which were held at her friend's house as she had a big living room. When I moved to Oxford in 1982 and then, later, to London, I continued to visit Juliet whenever I visited my parents.

Thirteen years after we first met, I had been telling Juliet about the three years I spent in an all-black women's psychotherapy group when she asked me if I would like to work with her. She called herself a healer. I didn't even know that's what she did. She believed that if you wanted to do some self-searching, it was better to have one-to-one sessions, rather than fight for attention within a group. I was pregnant with James when I started having sessions with her. She explained to me that I would have problems seeing my parents once I started working with her. I didn't know what she meant, but I soon found out. My parents were not too happy about the family laundry being aired in public. So I would drive the two hours to have my session with Juliet, then I would drive all the way back to London, bypassing my parents. One evening I bumped into my little brother, who was out with his mates, and I guess that didn't go down too well when he reported back to the parents.

I felt comfortable working with Juliet because she was in a mixed marriage and had mixed race children, like myself. From the first session I knew that what she did was what I wanted to do. I described working with her as butter melting in your mouth. She was kind and gentle and very soon, slowly but surely, things started to fall into place. I visited her whenever I could. It worked out every 6-8 weeks. I would get on with life and when something came up which I couldn't contain, I would make an appointment to go to Benson to see her. She helped me with my anger, so that I didn't take it out on Alistair. When James was born and I couldn't go in person, she gave me sessions on the phone. She introduced me to Louise Hay and I bought her book *You Can Heal Your Life*. In the book, I came upon a sentence that said that we choose our parents. This is what it said: "We come to this planet to learn particular lessons that are necessary for our spiritual evolution. We choose our sex, our colour, our country, and then we look around for the perfect set of parents who will 'mirror' our patterns." These sentences really enraged me. I remember raising what I had read on my next visit to see Juliet. I was so angry that I could have slapped her there and then, but she merely smiled and moved on with the discussion. So there started my search for why I would have chosen my parents, because I was perplexed. And if I had chosen them, then why did I hate them so much?

I continued to have sessions with Juliet until my son was 18, because I knew something was gravely wrong with *my* life. I wanted to get to the bottom of it so that I could be happy. I poured my heart out to her, and she helped me to uncover another way of being, a spiritual way. She gave me hope of a life that was possible, and in my reach, if I wanted it. She kept saying it was me, it was my fault, I had to stop reacting to situations and instead learn to respond. I understood what she was saying, but I didn't know what I was doing wrong. It was so inherent in me to behave the way that I was behaving. She also encouraged me to attend her yoga classes again, which I did every week for many years. She lectured for an hour on Buddhism, and then did yoga for an hour. This became my lifeline. It was all that made sense to me; it was what I was craving. I was getting a glimpse of this new way of living, but I wanted to live my life like this all the time, like Juliet did. That was my goal.

The class started at 10am, so I used to leave home before 8am to make the two-hour drive there and the two-hour drive home. I was shattered when I arrived home and would sleep for a further two hours. I was lucky because I was still working part-time at King's College Hospital and I never put myself forward to work on a Friday. Fridays were my yoga days. When James was nearly eighteen, I decided to give up this commute to Benson every Friday and find something closer. I also needed to do something else, career wise. I didn't want to be a kept woman all my life. So I opted to do an Access to Nursing course, which got me onto a midwifery course at King's College in Waterloo.

All the time I was seeing Juliet, I wondered why everyone wasn't queuing up to see her, as I used to tell all my friends how brilliant she was and how she was helping me to change my life. But, looking back, I realise how mad I was to do what I was doing, and that not everyone is so eager to look at their past like I was. That was all I wanted to do. I didn't know how to do anything else. I think of Juliet, and the love and patience she showed me, every day of my life. I will remember her always, how she would include me in her family activities. I am so grateful that I met her when I did and for the work we did together. She retired in 2018 and moved away and started a new life. She was from the school of thought that you never look back – something I have not yet perfected, but I am working on it.

~~~

Ranjanie

Two weeks after I stopped working with Juliet, I bumped into Ranjanie, who had been born into a Buddhist family in Sri Lanka. During those two weeks since leaving Juliet, I had worried about how I was going to cope alone. Due to stress, I had taken some time out of my midwifery course. To pass the time I decided to volunteer for Home Start, a local charity that supports families that are struggling. It was the first day of my training, but I had also booked to go to see the ballet *Swan Lake* in Covent Garden with Southwark Circle, an over 50s group that I belonged to. I managed to excuse myself from the training at the lunch break, and cycled all the way to Covent Garden from East Dulwich. I don't think I have ever cycled so fast, but I arrived in time for the 2pm start. I collected my ticket from one of the group representatives, then went upstairs to the circle to find my seat and my group. I found my seat, but none of my group were anywhere to be seen. I turned to a little Asian woman sitting next to me and asked her if she was with Southwark Circle. "No," she replied, "I am with Chelsea." It seemed she had also been separated from her group. Anyway, we got into conversation and soon started talking about meditation, as I was attending a twelve-week meditation course to relieve my stress. Then, out of the blue, she said to me, "Your guides sent you here today so that we could meet; my guides are always setting up meetings like this for me. I am going to be helping you on the next part of your journey."

It would be an understatement to say that I was shocked. This is the moment in the story of my life when I should have excused myself, gone to the ladies', and jumped out of the window. But I didn't. I merely sat where I was, taking it all in, totally numb. Just as well the ballet started and we couldn't talk anymore. All sorts of thoughts were swirling around in my head. I knew on one level that she was right. You read about these sorts of things happening in books or in films, but you never expect them to happen to you. I was watching the ballet, but my mind was somewhere else.

In the intervals we talked some more, and afterwards we went for a coffee in Cafe Nero across the road and continued talking until late. I didn't even bother to check up on my group. Ranjanie, the Asian woman, said that I was opening up spiritually and gave me lots of information about what to read and videos to watch. We exchanged e-mails and she continued to send me more stuff to read in our interactions. Too much really for me to read and process. I am still reading some of the stuff to this day. If I had a question (and I had many), I was able to ring her. We spent many hours on the phone in those early days and she didn't want any money for her time. She said her life purpose was to help people that were ready to open up.

We would meet in town for coffee. We also met at the Mind, Body and Spirit Festival at Olympia. She encouraged me to try different things. "Why don't you have a medium reading?" she said. I had an aura reading, and a photograph taken of my aura. In the photograph I was surrounded by the colour purple, which meant that I was a natural healer. She said she had thought so. She introduced me to some of her other students that she was supporting on this journey; one of them I am very close to and we speak regularly. The three of us would often meet up on Saturday mornings at the London Sangha, a Buddhist Monastic Order who follow the teachings of Thich

Nhat Hanh and practice mindfulness meditations.

I do not need the same constant support from Ranjanie as I used to, but I will still ring her for a chat, or text her with my latest news. And she still sends me stuff to read from time to time. She was prolific in getting me to where I am today, and for that I am very grateful to her for seeing something in me that needed nurturing.

~~~

Monica

I met Monica in September 2012 when I started my midwifery course. We were both students and were put in the same placement group at King's College Hospital. When we first met, I remember she said that I looked like her family. We were both black and had dreadlocks, and we were very mature students. We hit it off immediately. But very early on I was struggling. Just as I started the midwifery course, my son left to go to university up in Durham. That Christmas, my daughter also announced that she was leaving home to live with friends. She came home one day, said she was moving out, went upstairs, packed her bags and left. This had all been arranged with the help of her dad. I was devastated. I felt like I had already lost one child, and now the other one was leaving. I had exams at the beginning of January but I wasn't able to take them; I had to take time out from the course. And then in June 2014, my grandmother, who had brought me up, died, and then our beloved cat Salem died. It seemed to be one thing after the other. It was too much for me. I had been holding in too much and this was the cause of my first breakdown.

Monica had suggested that I start to chant. The very first meeting she took me to was at The Brixton Centre, and I remember it was a women's meeting. Some women had brought their children. When they started to chant, I was enthralled. It took me back to being little and playing around the mothers as they worked. I was captivated and felt I was home. I attended another meeting at the centre, and then a few meetings at a member's house. Monica told me there was a women's summer course coming up, but she couldn't go because she was going on a family holiday. I said I could go, so she gave me the details and I found myself on the weekend of the course taking the Metropolitan line all the way to Chalfont & Latimer. When I arrived, there was transport to take me to the hotel, De Vere Latimer, where I met loads of female Buddhists. There were a few faces I recognised from the few meetings I had been to, and they took care of me. I was also introduced to my local group and they asked me to hang out with them, which I did. It was a truly fabulous weekend. I met so many beautiful, brave and amazing women, and we spent the weekend studying, chanting, chatting, swimming and eating delicious food that the hotel prepared for us. After that weekend, I continued to attend my local group meetings. Although I already knew a lot about Buddhism, Nichiren Buddhism was new to me and so was chanting. As I settled into my new Buddhist family, I also knew that there was a lot of work to be done.

When I began to write about Monica, I hit a brick wall because I hadn't spoken to her for over nine months. I hit depression last summer and she had contacted me, but I hadn't answered her text. She came around a few days later and found me in a really bad way. I didn't even have food in the house. She was so shocked that I had allowed myself to sink so low. She gave me some money in an envelope, and went to the shops and bought me food. She came back and dumped it and said to me that I had to get my act together. "Life is for living," she told me, and then she left and didn't contact me again. Although I was out of the woods and feeling much better, I still hadn't had the guts to contact her to thank her for her love and kindness when I most needed it. She told me later that she was not prepared to watch me self-destruct, so she left me to it. Writing this book has given me the courage to contact her and carry on our relationship. I was able to return the money she had given me. She is now a grandmother.

Reflection

This chapter reveals to me that, each step of the way, I have been at the right place when I met the mentors who took it upon themselves to show me the next part of my journey. It has shown me that I was always held, or protected, as us Buddhists say. But like it says in the quote at the beginning of the chapter, I – the student – was ready to learn the lessons. Also, I do not think it is coincidence that all three of my mentors were Buddhists.

"What does attaining Buddhahood mean for us? It does not mean that one day we suddenly turn into a Buddha or become magically enlightened. In a sense, attaining Buddhahood means that we have securely entered the path, or orbit, of Buddhahood inherent in the cosmos. Rather than a final static destination at which we arrive and remain, achieving enlightenment means firmly establishing the faith needed to keep advancing along the path of absolute happiness limitlessly, without end."

Daisaku Ikeda

Chapter 6:
What My Three Mentors Taught Me

"People will forget what you said, people will forget what you did. But people will never forget how you made them feel."

Maya Angelou

Juliet

This morning, while doing yoga, I was thinking about my writing day ahead. It is Wednesday, and usually by this time I have finished my mind map and written at least two pages. But not this week. It seemed a mountain to climb to write about how my three mentors helped me, and how I took that wisdom on, and how it transformed me. As I was in the midst of doing my yoga postures, I thought – well, Juliet introduced me to yoga when I was twenty. Yoga was something new to me and I was good at it and enjoyed it. Because of this, since I moved to London I have always attended yoga classes. It's only recently in the last couple of years that I began to think to myself, "I do yoga every day. Why not do something more and train to be a yoga teacher?" I am always hearing friends complaining about their aches and pains, and not being able to find a good yoga teacher. I could be that person! I did the yoga course as a way of healing my life. I have now completed the course, and I have one client, who is also a friend. So Juliet introducing me to yoga has transformed me to a point where I am able to share my love of yoga with others, and yoga is a part of my daily life. Juliet also taught me about Buddhism, as she combined her yoga classes with lectures on Buddhism.

The last thirty years have been extremely challenging concerning my spiritual journey. It was very tough the majority of the time. I was in such pain; excruciating pain that would come and stay for hours, days, weeks or sometimes months. I would liken it to a black cloud that would park itself above my head and would not budge for love or money. I was trying to get my head around the fact that I was the one causing myself this pain. It was my pain, orchestrated by me. I kept reading my self-help books, keeping my diary, boring anyone who would listen to me, having my therapy sessions, going to the Buddhism/yoga classes. Sometimes I would do the Buddhism/yoga class for two hours, then go straight into a two-hour therapy session. In fact, I spent all my spare money on trying to heal my life. But the pain that was within me kept raising its head. What kept me going was the belief that through all this work I was doing, things had to get better; they just had to.

My thirties were shit, and so were my forties; it was in the latter part of my fifties that I began to see glimpses of a light at the end of the tunnel. I knew there was no turning back now. I even said to myself, "Even if I die trying, then so be it." All I knew was that I had to get rid of this pain that was inside me. Whatever it took, this was my life purpose. Before I consciously became aware that I was on this journey, most of the time I was hiding my feelings, and they would explode, unknowingly to me and when I least expected them to.

Juliet helped me to explore where my pain was coming from and why. After a session with her, I always felt much better, much calmer. I wanted so much to be able to deal with the situations in my life like she did. I couldn't get enough of her. I knew I was so lucky to have her in my life. She discouraged us from writing down any of the lessons when she lectured on Buddhism. She encouraged us to listen and said we would remember what we needed to remember. I am surprised that I have remembered so much of what she taught us.

Juliet encouraged me to keep a diary; to write down the stuff that was going on in my life. She said this would help me to feel better and I could keep an account of what to talk to her about when I saw her. When I complained that I sometimes could not sleep at night, she encouraged me to get up, whatever time it was, and write in my diary. I was worried about doing this, as I thought if I didn't get enough sleep, I would not be very productive the following day. She assured me that would not be the case. She was right – the release that my writing brought gave me the energy to get through the day on very little sleep. The times I wrote in the early hours were my most profound bits of writing. I have heard that the early hours are the times when we can most connect with our soul, so even to this day, I relish these early morning writing episodes.

Juliet introduced me to Inner Child work. In my sessions, she helped me to visualize going back to visit little Maggie, aged five, and say sorry that I hadn't visited her in a while. I would go back and knock on the door of our house back in Malawi and take her by the hand and walk to the swing at the bottom of the garden and push her on the swing. We would spend some time together chatting, then I would say goodbye to her and that I would see her again soon. At first I found these visualisations difficult, but I soon became comfortable doing this and looked forward to them. These days, I will take Little Maggie for a walk, go for an ice cream, go to the sweet shop and buy her favourite sweets or we will go to the cinema together. These trips are always very enjoyable; just the two of us, spending time together.

Juliet also introduced me to visualisation – bringing the person's face in front of me, so I could tell them what I wanted to say. I did this with my mum and dad. It was emotional and very powerful. I remember I had a lot of resistance at first.

She introduced me to putting a huge bubble around me to protect myself when I was feeling low. This bubble could be as big as I wanted it to be and it had all my favourite things in it.

Mine had loads of fluffy cushions and a large swing, which I would play on for hours and hours. The most important thing was that no one could get in and I could stay in it for as long as I liked. This is also an exercise I use from time to time if I can't sleep. I get myself all comfortable in my bubble and breathe deeply until I fall asleep. This has saved me many times when I have been depressed.

Very early on, Juliet introduced me to dream work as a way of starting the session. She would ask me if I had a dream to share with her, and I usually had, so she would decipher my dream. Apparently, having a dream is like receiving a personal letter in the post. You would not leave the letter unopened, would you? Dreams are the same; they are meant to be dissected and understood. Dreams are important because they inform us of what is going on in our subconscious mind, in the present moment. Anyone that appears in our dream is merely mirroring to us something we need to know. When you dream about someone, it is what that person represents to you that is important, not the person necessarily. It is up to us to take heed and try to understand the representation or ignore it as we wish. From dissecting my dreams, there was enough material to last us the whole session, so there was always something to talk about. Here is one example.

~~~

My brother Paul has died. Stricken with grief for him, I am devastated when they come and take his stuff away. They say I can't have it, that it doesn't belong to me. I am chasing them down the road as they carry his things away from his house – I am pleading with them not to take them away, saying I haven't even had time to look at them. I need time to look at them. In amongst all this, someone reverses against a 'No Parking' post. It's as if they can't see the post. They keep reversing back and back. A woman comes out of the shop she is working in to have a look at her car, which was parked next to the post, to see if it's okay. Then she disappears back inside the shop, when she sees that her car is not damaged by any of this.

~~~

After this dream, I woke up with a start at 5am and couldn't get back to sleep. I knew this dream was significant. I knew that the part of me that Paul represented was dead. Also, my relationship with a good friend of mine had come to an abrupt end when I tried to point out a flaw in our relationship, which had been going on for some time. I had finally managed to pluck up the courage to point it out to her but she wouldn't hear me. She shouted me down, saying I was trying to put the blame on her for something that had happened between me and another friend. She was having none of it, and she cancelled coming to birthday celebrations for her and another friend. This friend had befriended my friend Maureen, but she kept going through me every time she wanted to tell Maureen something. All I said to her was that she shouldn't come through me to tell Maureen something; in future, she should ring or text Maureen. She had Maureen's number and had rung her previously. But by saying this, I was taking away her control, her power, and this had been too frightening for her.

It also reminded me of the episode I had with my brother Paul a few weeks before, when he was trying to control how I grieved for our mother. I had continued to post things on our family WhatsApp group about what was going on in my life but then he sent me a private message saying, "What do you think you are doing? We are supposed to be mourning our mother." The catalyst was when I went to visit my son in Glasgow and I posted some photos of us climbing a Munro. Paul went mad and threatened to disband the group or leave. He ended up leaving the group.

Both my friend and Paul represented a side of me that was bossy, manipulative, didn't want to change, and was adamant on hanging onto my pain despite the fact that it was making me sick. This dream was showing me that I was letting go of that side of me. It was a huge moment for me. I didn't have to fix things anymore. I could just be with it until it panned itself out. My brother's stuff – I wanted to hang onto my past manipulative behaviours. I was so used to them, it was painful for me to let them go. I was letting go of what no longer served me.

I had this next dream the morning after I had finished typing out my book, 16th November, six and a half months after I started to write it.

~~~

I am in the house I am living in now and I've had a new baby boy. Lonie and James are in the room, and a Buddhist friend who has been practising for over thirty years, so has a lot of knowledge, is also there. This baby is tiny, as long as from my hand to my elbow. I ask James where he is, and he has put him by the window. I say to James, "We need to put the baby somewhere where he is safe and warm," and I put him on the pillow on the sofa with the alarm next to him. My friend says she is not leaving until she has cooked me something. So I am preparing to leave the baby with James while my friend and I go into the kitchen next door to cook. I pick up the baby's bonnet and another piece of clothing for me to rinse out and dry quickly on the radiator, so it can keep the baby's head warm. I feel Lonie's presence in the dream, but she does not play an active part; just James.

~~~

I woke up at 4.30am after having had this dream. I knew I had to write it down before I forgot it. A new baby means rebirth; I am beginning a new life. James represents a good friend, someone who cares about me, someone I look up to. He is a good sounding-board, someone I trust. He has a good head on him. He always sees both points of view. My Buddhist friend is someone I talk things over with when I am feeling overwhelmed and don't know which way to turn. She talks me through things until I can decide for myself which way to turn. She has come to feed me nourishment. Lonie is a divine presence guiding me; I just know she is there and this gives me the courage to carry on.

This dream shows me that by finishing typing out my book, I have entered a new phase of my life, a beautiful new phase and I have everything that I need on board to carry me through this next phase. The baby boy represents that I am coming into my male energy. I can take care of myself.

Juliet would always go on to us about minding our own business. She would say that we had enough business of our own to mind, without getting involved in other people's business. Lessons like these, you have been hearing them your whole life, but they take years and years to sink in on a profound level.

She would teach us about taking care of our taxes; making sure that all our affairs are taken care of. This meant making sure that all our bills are paid, and that we have written our Will. These were our affairs to be put in place by us. In other words, taking responsibility for our lives.

She used to tell us this story of the master and servant. The servant comes to the master and says, "Master, how can I become enlightened like you?" The master replies, "Take this glass of wine (which was full to the brim) and walk around the whole of my kingdom without spilling a drop. Then you will become enlightened." I used to imagine the servant going around the kingdom with this glass of wine, and the intensity that it would take to do this. To achieve this goal, he would really have to train his mind to be in the moment and not to stray. I didn't understand it at the time, but it is such a powerful story about how to live our lives in mindfulness.

Another favourite teaching she used to teach us was to 'be the captain of your ship'. She likened our lives to a ship, and the huge responsibility and intensity that a captain of a ship is under to protect the passengers on board his vessel. He cannot for a moment take his eye off the ball. He has to be in the moment at all times, or else he would get into big trouble. She was teaching us that is how we have to behave in our lives. Take ourselves seriously at all times. Again, I didn't understand it then, but I do now.

My favourite story that Juliet used to tell us was the story of Source. Every week she would bring in a huge illustration that she had drawn at home describing the lesson. In this one she had drawn in the sky a huge yellow cloud, which she described as Source. She said that each one of us is broken off from Source. We all come from Source; it is our home, which is all-loving, unconditional love. We all have a piece of Source energy within us for us to use, and if we run out and need to be replenished, we only have to ask and Source will give us more energy. Each of us has chosen to come to earth to experience duality. Earth is the only planet where we can experience duality – negativity and positivity. We learn our lessons through negativity. But because we come from Source, we are all powerful, whatever lesson we choose to come to earth to learn; we have the power to turn any negative experience into a positive one when we remember who we are. We have the power to remember that we are spiritual beings having a human experience. When we remember who we are, we know that whatever situation we may find ourselves in, we only have to ask for assistance from the angels and guides that are always there to guide us. We connect to Source by raising our vibrational levels through meditation. When we are in this state, we only have to ask and our prayers will be answered. But we have to be patient and wait for the answer. Not many of us have the patience to wait, so we miss the signposts to what we desire.

Juliet often talked about relationships. The importance of being a whole person wanting to have a relationship with another whole person; not taking extra baggage into a relationship. That is why it was so important for us to work on ourselves and not blame anyone else for why our life was not working. That is why I have not entered into another relationship following my divorce. I chose to work on myself first until I am whole.

Juliet also taught us the importance of looking ahead in life and not looking back. She suggested that when we want a rest, we should take a holiday in the garden, not get on a plane and go abroad, because that is very stressful, and you usually need a holiday when you return to get over the stress. She taught me many, many other things, but these are what instantly come to mind.

~~~

Ranjanie

When I first met Ranjanie, she bombarded me with so much information to read. Orin and DaBen, Masters of the Spirit World, John Newton, Emanuelle McIntosh, Tina Louise Spalding, Roberta Grimes, Toni Winninger to name a few. I particularly liked Orin and DaBen and Masters of the Spirit World and concentrated on these. She taught me about our thoughts becoming our reality and to be mindful of my thoughts. If I feel a negative thought arising, to cancel it out, and replace it with a positive thought. This is where affirmations and positive self-talk became important. I would write affirmations and positive self-talk sentences on revision cards and stick them around the house, where I could easily see them to remind myself to stay on the positive track. I also made a vision board with a lot of positive sentences about how I wanted my life to look, and I put it on my bedroom wall and would spend some time reading them out loud, to keep myself on track. Louise Hay is very good for positive affirmations, and Shad Helmstetter's book *What to Say When You Talk to Your Self* is very good for positive self-talk; their phrases would be going around and round in my head all day long. Sometimes, I would exhaust myself so I would just shut down my brain.

Ranjanie taught me about gratitude. She taught me to be grateful every day for what you have; then the Universe will send you more things to be grateful for. If you are negative, the

Universe will send you more negativity. I would write down ten things every day that I was grateful for. In the early days, when I couldn't think of ten things, I wouldn't beat myself up about it. But now I have no problem finding ten things to be grateful for. You start to look at the simple things in life, like being grateful for a walk, or spending time in nature, hearing birdsong. Doing these daily exercises raises our vibrational levels, connecting us to our soul, thus receiving instructions from our soul instead of our mind. When we follow our soul, we are on track to living our life purpose. When you raise your vibrational level, everything starts going your way; life begins to work.

I must add that it took a few years for me to perfect this. I would start and stop, start and stop, because at times it would be very difficult to work on doing the affirmations and positive self-talk every day. Sometimes I would be too tired, and my brain couldn't think any more. Then, after a few days or weeks, I would get back on it again, as I knew it was important for my spiritual growth and I had Ranjanie supporting me, telling me I was nearly there and that I was doing so well. I also had my chanting and yoga, which I was doing daily as well. I began to realise how happy I was when my vibrational level was high, but it could so easily drop if I was not vigilant – it involved daily work.

Ranjanie taught me about forgiveness, and the importance of sending love and light to everyone, especially family, every day. Every day I learnt to say to my family: "I love you, I respect you, I am sorry, I trust you and I thank you for all the lessons you have taught me. You have taught me acceptance, charity, compassion, confidence, courage, empathy, faith, forgiveness, generosity, gratitude, hope, joy, kindness, laughter, love, patience, perseverance, respect, tolerance and trust, and I only have gratitude for you. I thank you for pressing my buttons, so that I could learn the lessons I have come to learn in order to fulfil my life purpose." In my private prayers I ask the Universe to give me the power, strength and wisdom to learn the lessons that I have come to learn and to fulfil my life's purpose. I pray for the members of my family to be well and thank them for all the lessons they have taught me, especially my mum. And every day in my prayers I send special love and gratitude to Mum and Lonie for agreeing to be my mother and daughter and for helping me to learn the lessons that I planned to experience on earth this lifetime as Maggie.

She taught me that nothing is right, nothing is wrong. It's only an experience on Planet Earth as a human being. She taught me that we have a meeting with our soul family in which we plan our life before we are born, depending on the lessons we wish to learn this lifetime. Nothing that happens to us is by chance. The people in our life who press our buttons, especially our family, are playing to the script that we asked them to play so we could learn a lesson that we wished to learn. It is up to us to learn the lesson that a particular individual is trying to teach us. Once we have learnt the lesson, that individual can no longer press our buttons, and we can move on to the next lesson, lesson complete. Our purpose as humans on earth is to experience life in duality, through positivity and negativity, and, through these experiences, evolve. It is that simple. When we as humans come to earth, we suffer amnesia and forget the reason why we are here. Also, if the family we are born into do not nurture our uniqueness, it can take us a long time to remember who we are and why we have come to earth this lifetime. Some people never remember, and will leave without realizing their full potential. These souls will probably have to come back and relearn the lessons again. We are spiritual souls having a human experience. It is not personal, but so many of us, including me, make it so.

Ranjanie advised me to take on board the teachings only if they resonated with me. I loved learning about this stuff. I couldn't get enough of it. In the beginning I would ring her, ask to meet her, so that she could repeat them again and again. This new language that I was learning really resonated with me. It was what I had been dying to hear, because I understood that it was innate in me. I knew I was on my way to fulfilling my life purpose. I knew I was on the way to releasing all the pain I had harboured all my life. These were exciting times for me, when I caught glimpses of what I could become. There was still a lot of pain to plough through. She taught me meditation and sent me meditation tapes. She never gave up on me. That was important for me.

I already had the gift of chanting in my life, another form of meditation. Chanting is my time to go within and embrace all that inhabits my mind. I make my 'to do list' while chanting. Then I can guarantee that my day will go swimmingly.

Ranjanie taught me how to connect with my guides. She explained to me that we have one guide who is always with us, but other guides are available to us as well. We have to remember to ask for the help, and look for the signposts. With her guidance, I learnt to talk to them and to ask them what the pain is that I am feeling, and await their reply. I found that when I started to confront the pain, it would disappear. The pain merely wanted my attention, acknowledgement that it was there. I learnt how to connect with my Higher Self, how to ask my Higher Self for help. As a way of remembering, I tied a long string on a Christmas bauble and suspended it to the curtain rail, and every morning when I wake up and every evening when I am going to sleep, I push it a few times, as you would push a swing, and thank it, my Higher Self, for everything that it is teaching me.

Ranjanie taught me to respect beggars and the journey they are on. Before, I never quite knew how to behave when I saw beggars. I would tense up. These days I know to appreciate the journey that they are on and I say a prayer asking the Universe to give them the power, the strength and the wisdom to learn the lessons that they have come to learn, and to fulfil their life purpose. Sometimes I will give them money, but I do not feel the guilt that I once did around them. I will even hold a conversation with them to find out where they are on their journey.

~~~

Monica

Monica introduced me to Nichiren Buddhism in 2014. I was not a stranger to Buddhism, but chanting was new to me. She invited me to my first Buddhist meeting, and subsequent meetings. Although I belonged to a different group to her, she would often invite me to meetings in her group. She taught me the importance of chanting every day, morning and evening, to reap the benefits. Study was also important – reading some Buddhist text for twenty minutes every day, and sharing the practice with others, so that they too could become happy. She showed me by example, the way she lived her life and wholeheartedly believed in taking whatever troubles she had to the Gohonzon (the scroll we chant to.) She and her twin sister Michelle had been practising for twenty-five years. I would say to myself, "They have been practising for 25 years; there must be something in it." I would also think this when I attended meetings and met others who were devoted to chanting. I was totally ready for this.

Reflection

I was struggling this week, so I wrote myself a letter to read in a few weeks to encourage myself. It went like this:

Dear Maggie

By the time you get to this day, the 7th September 2020, you will have completed the first draft of your book, and you will be well on your way to being a published author. Well done you, is all I can say. It is no longer a dream but a reality, and you have made that reality come true. How cool is that? But also, this is not a time to become complacent; for there is still a lot of work to be done. The next stage is to type up each chapter and make any amendments you would like to make. I think you are going to enjoy the next stage, Maggie, because you enjoy typing, and you are going to be typing your own work. It doesn't get any better than that, does it?

I think the halfway stage was a bit wobbly for you; as you described, it felt like you were swimming in the middle of the Channel. You could no longer see Dover behind you, and Calais was not yet in sight. You wondered what you were doing, swimming, feeling tired, wishing for familiar ground. But deep down in your heart, you also knew that you just had to keep swimming until you could see land ahead. But now, as you embark on chapter 10 tomorrow, I can see you are feeling more comfortable in yourself, more determined. Your friend Maureen has said your writing gets better every week. She is not just saying that, she means it. She is your number one fan, I think, don't you?

So keep resting at the weekends, keep jotting down the thoughts that go through your mind, ready to include them in your writing. Keep having those walks around the cemetery, keep meeting up with your walking buddies. They are sustaining you in a way that you cannot comprehend at this time. Keep e-mailing Ellen to keep her posted on how you are feeling. You are doing great. I am rooting for you – and remember that your guides and your angels are also there, waiting to assist you. You only have to ask. So enjoy the process as much as the goal, Maggie.

See you on the 7th September, first draft completed.

Your best friend,

Maggie

~~~

I will not lie, it was tough revisiting all those lessons my mentors taught me; some of them took me years to grasp. There were good times, but there were also some dark times I had to wade through, not always having the knowledge that I have now, and the belief that everything was going to be alright. I have never forgotten how these three women made me feel. They were all very kind, loving and compassionate and instilled in me how special I was. Because of them, I try every day to emulate the lessons they taught me to everyone that I meet.

"The deepest place on Earth is not a physical place, but the stillness we enter at the bottom of our pain, at the bottom of our fear and worry. The stillness we enter there opens us to a spacious state of being that some call joy."

Mark Nepo

Chapter 7:
Ellen

"We create our own reality. The world is just an illusion. Anything is possible. Miracles can and do happen, if we are willing to stop struggling and allow them into our lives. Like the White Queen, we should perhaps make a habit of believing as many as six impossible things before breakfast."

Gill Edwards

I first met Ellen, who is coaching me to write this book, in 2014, the May Bank Holiday, at The Mind, Body and Spirit Festival at Olympia. I had been to this festival some time ago on my search for spiritual matters. This time I was there because Ranjanie had encouraged me to come. She said it is a beautiful place for spirituality and the energies there are very high. While she was volunteering with her Reiki group, I had the opportunity to walk around on my own. I remember being in a daze, working hard at avoiding eye contact with vendors who all had something they wanted to sell me.

I turned the corner and there was Ellen with her book in her hand, asking me if I wanted to buy it, and she continued with the blurb. I remember she was beautifully made up and engaging and she had the most beautiful smile to match. It was difficult to avoid her. The book she was promoting was *Cosmic Ordering Made Easier: How to Get More of What you Want, More Often.* I had never heard of this concept before, but as she started to explain it to me, I felt that it might be something I would be interested in. I didn't have £14.99 on me, which was the cost of the book, but she asked me if I wanted to write on a postcard something that I wanted to happen in three months' time and put my name and address on it; she would send it to me in three months' time, and I could see whether it had manifested. I was happy to do this.

Three months later, the card appeared on my doorstep. I can't remember what I had written; the most important thing is it prompted me to buy the book and start cosmic ordering. In the book, Ellen says it is important to write down your order so that you recognise it when it arrives, and to look out for the signposts, which I started to do. From time to time I picked up the book, made a few more orders, wrote them down and continued to live my life.

Fast-forward to the beginning of 2019 and looking to plan the new year ahead. I wanted to start up my own business, helping people to live their life purpose, and I was looking to get a small business loan from Virgin. But I was lacking confidence that I could really do this. I picked up Ellen's book and started to read it again. This led me to look up the cosmic orders I had made previously. A couple of years before, on 7th October 2016, I had made an order for a new garden fence. I'd been looking down the garden at my poor fence, which was probably as old as my Victorian house, and I placed an order that went: "What I really want is to have my garden fence mended and I don't want to pay anything for it for the good of all concerned." I looked down the garden now to see my brand new, intact fence. New neighbours had moved in next door, renovated the whole house and provided me with a new fence – and they didn't want any money for it, although we had previously agreed to go halves. "Wow, this stuff really does work," I thought. There were a few others that had also manifested. (Later you'll read a whole chapter about my cosmic ordering stories.)

So, in January 2019, I was wondering if Ellen did workshops. I looked at her website and realised that I had just missed one that weekend. When I looked further, I saw she did workshops once a month, so I booked to go to the February workshop. My brother lives in Swindon, near where Ellen lives, so I asked him if I could stay with him the night before. He agreed, although he wasn't too pleased about it, as he had recently returned from Malawi and wanted to get on with his work. He refused me a lift to Ellen's house on the morning of the workshop, so I took a taxi and was there on time at 10am. There was me and another woman there. We had a beautiful day, working, taking breaks, wandering around the garden for inspiration. It was nice to meet the author of the book again and have a first-hand insight into some of the things she had written about such as the driveway for her cars, and the plants she rescued that her husband's office were going to throw away. Her husband Rich kept us fed and watered throughout the day, and later he kindly gave me a lift to the station. It had been a truly inspiring day, and I loved the way Ellen went about solving problems. I remember saying to Ellen that day that I wanted to write a book about my cosmic ordering stories. She had replied, "Great, I am starting my own publishing company, so I will be able to help you publish it if you want." I didn't think any more about this as I continued with my life, working at starting up my own business and planning a trip to Malawi for my brother's 60th birthday.

I must add at this point that a particular quote in Ellen's book had caught my attention:

"Until you make the unconscious conscious,
it will direct your life and you will call it fate."

Carl G Jung

I love Jung, so I loved this quote. I also noticed that Ellen had written this quote twice to highlight its significance. Throughout my life my dad, who loved Freud, had shoved him down my throat. But I always rejected Freud. He just didn't resonate with me. When I was at university I encountered Jung, and loved him. He totally resonated with me. He made so much sense to me. Jung and Freud were great friends. In fact, Jung says that Freud was the father figure he did not have in his own father. But there came a time when Jung knew in advance of the publication of his book about the libido that it would cost him his friendship with Freud. He knew that everything was at stake, but he resolved to go ahead and write it anyway. As a result he was ostracised from Freud's circles and Freud did not speak to him for ten years, which had a deep impact on him. This man really spoke to my soul, as this had also been my experience with my parents when I had started therapy, although I had been estranged from them for three years. The pain was just as great.

Ellen had found an explanation to this quote that she could understand in Lisa Cherry's book *Soul Journey*. Ellen thanked Lisa and Carl for this insight. I wanted to know who this Lisa Cherry was. I searched for her book on Amazon but it was £45! I thought, "What sort of book is this? I can't afford that sort of money." But this year, I searched for it again and found a copy for £20. "That's better," I thought, and I bought it. I read it very quickly. I loved Lisa' story and the stories of the other women included in the book. As I read through the bibliography at the back of the book, I thought to myself, "I have read most of these books here. I could write a book about my life." It was something I had always wanted to do, ever since I was a child in Mrs Trowbridge's class, when she had caught me writing about my life in Malawi, but I had shied away in embarrassment. Rolling the clock forward fifty years, I thought, "If Lisa Cherry can do it, then so can I."

I arrived back from Malawi in August 2019 and suffered yet another breakdown when I went into voluntary lockdown. As I came out of it in January 2020, one of the things I thought about doing was writing that book. I sent Ellen an e-mail saying I was ready to write the book and asking her how much it would cost. I didn't hear from her, and when the Covid lockdown happened, I panicked as I didn't want to go down that depression route again. So I decided to put all my energy into completing a yoga course that I was doing by correspondence course. Up to this point I was doing two or three classes a week, and I had completed 70 hours out of the required 150. As soon as lockdown was announced, one of my yoga teachers got her act together and started offering yoga classes on Zoom three times a day for a donation. I was doing all the classes, seven days a week, so it took me no time at all to finish my 150 hours. Now I am three theory lessons away from becoming a yoga instructor. Doing so much yoga every day brought up a lot of emotional stuff for me, which I found difficult to contain. Talking to my yoga teacher about it, she suggested I log the changes I was going through as a yoga student. "Who knows what you might do with it afterwards," she said. "You maybe could write a book about your experiences." She also said to me, "The world needs what you have to offer, Maggie."

Around this time, I received an e-mail back from Ellen with a breakdown of her fees. As my yoga course was nearing its end, I panicked – what was I going to do now? so I decided I would take up Ellen's offer and write my book. Late one evening I found myself clicking the button saying 'Yes' to becoming a 'Published Author'. I realised during the VIP Day that I had misread the e-mail. I thought it was £650 for the whole thing, but that was just for the VIP Day, and then it was going to be £450 per month for the next six months until Christmas. I panicked yet again. I didn't have this sort of money. I wasn't even working. But Ellen said: "Let's cut this day short. Then at least you can afford June and let's not worry about July. In fact, you can put a cosmic order in for the rest of the money to come through." This not worrying about money thing was new to me. I always worried about money. Anyway, I decided to go with it, not to worry, put in a cosmic order for the money, and I started writing. By the time July came, I decided to use £1500 of my savings – all the money I had – to pay for July, August and September. I was prepared to do this because I was enjoying the process so much; getting up every morning with a purpose that I loved. I kept having this feeling at the back of my mind that I should be doing something else, that I was wasting my time. That was my ego mind talking. It was probably the mass consciousness and negativity that I had picked up along the way, but I knew that I was enjoying the writing, and having Ellen to talk to once a week to keep me on the straight and narrow was imperative to my success. The cosmic order would take care of the rest. By January 2021, my cosmic order for the rest of the money came through when I had a pension payout backdated for ten months from Barclays Bank, whom I had worked for six years back in my twenties. I would be able to complete writing my book after all.

Reflection

I was aware from the day I met Ellen that she was special, although I had been in a daze and I had no idea that our journeys would be so entwined again and again as they panned out. I, the student, took six years to become ready to accept her as my teacher. She has been there every step of the way, inspiring me to write my story and encouraging me that I had something to offer. I am so grateful that I followed the signs of my cosmic order to write my book. It is also encouragement to all of you out there that you can follow your dreams.

"Becoming a human does not mean that we must suffer until life is not worth living. The Masters are very clear that we do not have to be crushed by our experiences.
Our task is to learn the lessons that we have set for ourselves and to carry on intact spiritually.
No lesson is too much for the soul to tackle. We don't always learn easily and well. Earth is the toughest environment out there. But each one of us has chosen this fast track to knowledge and wisdom, and we get what we've asked for because over the rainbow,
skies really are blue."

Betty Shine

Chapter 8:
Susan

"We must present ourselves to the world and look at it as a great adventure."

Beatrix Potter

I met Susan in 1968 when I came to live in the UK. We met at Cholsey Primary School, which was then in Berkshire. She was in Mrs Robertson's class. I was in Mrs Trowbridge's class. The headmaster Mr Campbell and his wife ran the small village school. I remember Mr Campbell loved bird watching and would take out some of the boys who were interested in it. Obviously, everything was new to me and I was learning a new language. But I loved school. I loved everything about it. It was what saved me, I think, as things were not always easy at home. Those were also the days when we got a free bottle of milk to drink every day, which was delicious. Not everyone thought so, and I remember staying behind when school finished to have an extra bottle.

In the summertime, we had our playtimes in the field next to the playground, and we played rounders every single afternoon. I don't know how those children felt who didn't like rounders, but I loved it. I also loved sports day, when we did the egg and spoon race and the obstacle race, amongst others. I loved partaking in them all. Because the field was next to a brook, our balls were constantly going into the brook and we had to retrieve them, coming out with wet shoes and socks. Somehow, we never minded much. It was part of the fun, and the game had to go on.

I remember my last year at primary school with such

happiness. Mr and Mrs Campbell retired, and our new headmaster was called Mr Haworth. I remember he was very tall and had a moustache and a huge beard, which he liked to stroke. He was very kind and forward thinking. Across the brook a new building was being constructed which was going to house the last year of primary school. We were going to be the first year to use it. It was all very exciting. Mr Haworth had commanded that all the walls be taken down. He didn't want any walls in his school. So that's what happened. I have since found out that this idea was based on the Agora School in Roermond, Netherlands. The whole building became open plan. There were quiet rooms dotted about which were carpeted, so we had to take our shoes off when entering them. These rooms were used for morning and afternoon registration with our form teachers. They were also used for reading, or sitting in if you wanted to be quiet. Sometimes, our form teacher Mrs Dempster would request that we gathered together if she wanted to talk to us; otherwise, we were free to roam as we pleased. We had individual timetables, which we had to adhere to. We were each given so many pages of beta maths, creative writing, science and art. We could do this work in our own time, individually or in groups. My friends and I – including Susan – would arrive very early on Monday morning and get all our tasks done by the end of the day or maybe Tuesday morning. Then we would have the rest of the week to do exactly what we wanted to do. The teachers would organise different activities for us, and we were free to take part in any of these, or we could organise our own activities. The teachers were always on hand if we needed support. There were swimming trips to the local town in Wallingford. I remember one time Susan came back upset, because she had lost her pants. I never went swimming as I could not yet swim. One of the teachers, Mrs Lomax, put on a production of *A Midsummer's Night Dream*, which they performed outside at the end of our school year. My friend Lyndsey played Helena. It was so magical and by far the most beautiful thing I had ever seen. I remember my friend

Rosemary and I did assembly one morning. We were encouraged to do this. I can't remember what subject we chose. We also chose the hymns and for the length of the assembly, we held everyone's attention. It went well, but I do remember there being a few embarrassing pauses as we worked out what was coming next. I also remember us doing tree rubbings outside in the field in the summer months.

Talking to my primary school friend Lyndsey recently, (she now likes to be called Lyn) she remembers the building vividly, the colour of the carpets, the colour of the walls. She remembered us playing together, which I don't remember. She doesn't remember hanging out with anyone else but me, as she was shy and didn't make friends easily. She remembers how freeing our last year of primary school was, and what a shock it was when we went to secondary school. She remembers playing Helena in *A Midsummer's Night Dream*, walking on stage and forgetting her lines. She remembers sitting in the courtyard in the sun, working on her project.

At lunchtimes we didn't have to queue up for our food. We sat eight to a table, including one teacher per table. Two monitors were chosen each week to go up to the counter and collect the food in serving dishes and serve us our meal. Afterwards, they would clear away the plates and serve us our pudding. It was all very civilised.

As I have already said, every afternoon in the summer we played rounders, so you could say we were very good at it. One day, one of the teachers said that he had entered us for a rounders tournament the following week. There was no time to panic. I remember my mum had to buy me a pair of navy-blue shorts especially for the occasion. We went to our very first rounders tournament by coach. I remember we had the afternoon off school. At the tournament, we won game after game because we were so brilliant, and before we knew it, we were in the final. We didn't panic. For us, it was just like any afternoon playing rounders in our school field, and lo and behold, we came home with the cup. You could say that we were very pleased with our performance. We continued to play rounders until we left for secondary school, when everything became regimented again. That crazy last year of primary school was the only time that Susan and I were in the same class together during our school years.

At secondary school, we were in different forms, she in 1A and I in 1B. We hung out with our respective classmates, although sometimes we played together in the playground. Boys and girls had different playgrounds. There were so many changes to adhere to. One of them was being back to boxed classrooms; our freedom was over, so it seemed. But I must say that last year of primary school had a huge impact on me and my hunger to become a free spirit.

After the third year, our school went comprehensive, and we joined with the boys' grammar school down the road. I left school with 5 CSEs. I had rather given up on school because going comprehensive meant that we didn't have end of term examinations anymore, so I didn't know where I was. Before, we had exams so we knew our exact positions in our class. I had come top of my class that year, and in the old system, I would have automatically gone up a level and would have received an award in the end of term assembly in front of the whole school. I was upset, because my form teacher Mrs Quinn had already chosen who was going to receive the prize, but as a consolation, she said she would give me money to buy a book of my choice and she would sign it for me. I turned this offer down. It didn't seem fair somehow. As far as I was concerned, I didn't get my reward for working hard, and she wasn't going to pacify me in any way or form.

I left school at sixteen, not knowing what I was going to do with my life. I went to Oxpens College of Further Education in Oxford to do some O Levels. Susan also went, but she was doing a secretarial course. Again, we saw each other regularly, usually in the evenings. After leaving college, she got a secretarial job at Blackwell's Publishing Company, and I was working as a typist at Barclays Bank, after doing a secretarial course at Wilson's Secretarial School in Reading. I remember I worked in a factory for a few months in order to pay for the course. Susan and I would meet occasionally for lunch, as we were both working in Oxford. She travelled to work by train, but our family had by this time moved to Benson, where there was no longer a train station, so I took the bus to work. We did the usual things: went out for meals, travelled up to London for concerts, went to discos at the weekends at Top Rank in Reading. That was the place to go disco dancing in those days. My brothers were happy for me and my friends to tag along as long as we did not bother them once there. It wasn't cool to have a little sister tugging at your sleeve when you wanted to impress a girl, I guess.

Susan was mad about Donny Osmond. I remember she had a life-size photo of him on the landing in her house, because that was the only place it would fit. Talking to her recently, she was sure that I had travelled up to London with her once to see the Osmonds, but that was not me. I never saw the Osmonds. She was also crazy about the Bay City Rollers; I remember her favourite was Eric. I do remember going with her to The New Theatre in Oxford to see them though. I remember the screaming fans and the foyer upstairs being full of teenagers who had fainted, lying on the floor with the Red Cross Ambulance staff overstretched as they tried to revive them with smelling salts. I had never seen anything like it. I myself loved Michael Jackson, and Marty Kristian of The New Seekers. Gladys Knight and the Pips were also up there for me. I never did see Michael Jackson live, but I saw The New Seekers many times. I remember that I dragged Susan to see them once, and Lyndsey. I managed to see Gladys Knight just last year at the Royal Albert Hall for the first time. Now in her 70s, she has not lost any of her magic. The black pop stars on TV every Thursday evening on *Top of the Pops* were the only black faces I got to see, so there was a lot invested in them; such names as Diana Ross, The Jackson Five, The Chi-Lites, The Stylistics, The Four Tops, Sweet Sensations, to name a few. I also remember vividly black programmes like *Roots*, a documentary about Dr Martin Luther King, *Love Thy Neighbour*, and I especially loved Sidney Poitier in *Guess Who's Coming to Dinner*. At that time, there were no black footballers playing professional football. Having three brothers who were football mad, I had no choice really but to partake.

When Susan and I were 19, we saved up our money and went to Malawi for a month over Christmas. This was my first trip back since coming over in 1968, so I was somewhat apprehensive about flying. One lunchtime, while out shopping, I bumped into a group of Christians singing Christmas songs. They asked me if they could pray for me when I told them about my anxiety about flying to Malawi. They said a prayer for me, and my anxiety lifted. I also remember that my new passport had not arrived and we were due to fly out in a few days. My dad had contacted one of his friends at the Malawi Embassy, and lo and behold, my passport arrived the next morning and we were free to fly. It had been touch and go whether we would be able to go.

We had a beautiful trip to Malawi. Susan's aunt had lent us some beautiful dresses to wear on our trip, which was lovely. I saw my grandma again, but I could no longer converse with her because I had forgotten most of my Chichewa. It was lovely to see my aunts and uncles again after such a long time. On Christmas Day, my Aunt Tertia, who was heavily pregnant, gave birth to my cousin Chikondi, so Susan and I ended up making Christmas dinner for everyone. I remember it was the rainy season and some of the roads were quite muddy. Once we had to push the car because it got stuck in the mud, and our lovely dresses were all covered in mud. Another time, while we were visiting my grandma at the farm where I was raised, my uncles had taken us for a walk in the midday heat. Susan, being fair, was wearing a dress that exposed her back and she hadn't put any sun cream on. The next day, her back was covered in huge blisters. I must say, my uncles did panic a bit. They had never seen anything like it.

Now in our early twenties, Susan was preparing to marry her long-term boyfriend Charlie and move to Valencia in Spain, where his family were from. But first he had to do his National Service. Susan joined him in Valencia for the last part of it. Then they came back here for their wedding, before moving to Spain permanently. By this time, I had met Alistair. She wouldn't let me bring Alistair to the wedding as she only wanted people there that she knew, which was fair enough, although I was hurt. I got married three years later, but Susan couldn't come because she was heavily pregnant with her first son.

Throughout this time, something was changing; we were changing, our lives were changing. We were writing to each other, but even then, something was missing. It felt to me that Susan was repeating the same letter. There didn't seem to be anything new. So I stopped writing to her. Some time passed and I got a letter from her asking me why I hadn't written. What had she done wrong? So I wrote and told her exactly how I was feeling. It took twenty pages. I hadn't heard of therapists then. She refused to speak to me after that. I tried to write to her to apologise, but she was having none of it. I wanted her to know how I was feeling, but I didn't realise that it would end our friendship, but it did. I visited her once when she came to stay with her in-laws, before they retired to Spain. She had her two boys with her; they were very young. The meeting was strained.

In the spring of 1991, before Lonie was born, Alistair and I went to Valencia in the hope of seeing Susan. We managed to see her father-in-law and Charlie, her husband, but he was hostile and said Susan was preparing to take the boys away for a break. I was devastated because I really did miss her. I even sent her photos of my children when they were born, but I heard nothing back. The pain was so much. When I started therapy, I talked it over with my therapist, Juliet. She assured me that I had done nothing wrong, because she had asked me, and I had told her. When I could no longer endure the pain, I turned to God and said: "I can't deal with this anymore. I am handing it over to you, but I would like to see her one more time before I die," and this helped me tremendously to let her go. I would occasionally think of her, but the pain was not as bad. I would quickly move on.

In 2013, 34 years later, I received a message from Susan on Facebook: "Hi Maggie, I expect you are surprised to see me here on Facebook. I must say I don't use it very much but was very pleased to find you there. I know that a lot of things happened between us many years ago. However, I have never forgotten you and often wondered about you and your life. I know you have two lovely children. You must be very proud. My sons are well grown up now and I have just become a grandmother to a lovely girl called Daniella. Well, if you ever fancy chatting, I will be pleased to speak to you. Best wishes, Susan."

I was honestly shocked to get this message, because I had given up on ever hearing from her again. I had looked for her on Friends Reunited, to no avail. So we started to send messages back and forth on Facebook. I told her of my divorce and life as a single parent. She had just become a grandma and she was still married to Charlie. Six months into us speaking, she was diagnosed with cancer of the lymph nodes, and she spent 2014 fighting it. I sent her lots of encouragement, especially Louise Hay affirmations.

We didn't meet until the summer of 2015. She comes over every year to visit her parents in Bournemouth and this time, she passed through London and stayed with me overnight. Our first meeting was outside the front entrance of the Peter Jones store in Sloane Square. I remember I walked straight past her, as I was looking for a 23-year-old version of her; the last time I had seen her. We were now in our 50s. It was weird meeting her again after so long. There was so much to say and catch up on, and yet a lot of it didn't seem that important after such a passage of time. We had lunch in Peter Jones, then we made our way back to South London. I had made something for supper the night before, so I wouldn't spend my time cooking while she was there. My son was home from university and had supper with us. Then we spent the evening catching up. The next day, we took a train to London Bridge and walked all over London, looking at the sights. We stopped and had lunch at Wagamama's on the Embankment, then walked across Westminster Bridge to Trafalgar Square, through Leicester Square to Piccadilly Circus, to Regent Street and Oxford Street. Susan wanted to visit Balderton Street, just off Oxford Street and very near to Selfridges, as her grandmother had lived there on the top floor and worked as a housekeeper for a doctor. Susan's mum and aunt – twin sisters – were born there. Her mum weighed 3lb and her sister weighed 4lb. Apparently the midwife had looked at them, shaken her head and said they would not survive. It was nice to hear this story because this is a side of Susan that I did not know. She spent all the holidays in Balderton Street with her grandmother, until she died when Susan was 17. How cool is that? From Oxford Circus, we jumped on the tube to Victoria Station, where she took a coach to Bournemouth. It had been a really wonderful couple of days.

I have not only seen Susan once, but three times now. This year, 2020, would have been the fourth year. We were due to go and see *The Lion King* for our 60th birthdays, but it was cancelled because of Covid-19, and although she still came to visit her parents in Bournemouth, she decided not to come to London. We are planning to see *The Lion King* and celebrate our birthdays once lockdown restrictions are lifted.

Reflection

This quote by Betty Shine is what kept me going this week:

"I had not yet learned the most important lesson in life, which is that nothing would ever be finished without discipline. This is especially true if you want to be a writer, because it is a lonely and solitary life."

I have made many friends on my journey to enlightenment through the books that I have read. One such friend is Eckhart Tolle and his book, *The Power of Now*, in which he says that the past is gone, so why dwell on it; the future is not yet here, so why worry about it, because we might never get there. But it is the now, how we behave in the present moment, that changes our lives. In the present moment, we can choose to be positive or negative, and this decision will shape our future.

I am glad that I had the opportunity to put this teaching into practice when Susan and I reunited. I felt what had happened between us in the past was no longer relevant. Being positive and building a positive future became more important. I have also learnt that patience is important, and that sometimes it is best to let time do its healing.

Reading through this chapter has shown me that our friendship has come a long way, and it has taught me to treasure friendships more, especially old friendships.

Also, I had no idea how much my last year at primary school had shaped me into fighting all my life to become a free spirit.

"You get in life what you have the courage to ask for."

Oprah Winfrey

Chapter 9:
Identity Crisis

"During my lifetime I have dedicated myself to this struggle of the African people. I have fought against white domination, and I have fought against black domination. I have cherished the ideal of a democratic and free society in which all persons live together in harmony and with equal opportunities. It is an ideal which I hope to live for and to achieve. But if needs be, it is an ideal for which I am prepared to die."

Nelson Mandela

I don't remember my identity – the fact that I am black – being an issue while I was at primary school. I had fun and had loads of friends. I had the usual thing of the other kids being fascinated with my hair and wanting to touch it to see if it was real. There was the name calling of "wog" and "go back to where you came from", but my friends would always rally round and put a stop to it, and, like children, we would move on to something else. It never festered. There was one day when my oldest brother, who went straight to secondary school when we moved to this country, came home from school in tears because one of the neighbour's boys who was on the school bus with him had spat on his brand-new school coat. I remember my dad was so angry. He took the soiled jacket and knocked on the boy's door, spoke to the boy's mother and gave her the jacket and demanded she cleaned it, which she did. An incident like that never happened again, and my brother informs me that they were very good friends after that. My dad had nipped it in the bud.

Our dad taught us to get on with everyone, despite the

colour of their skin. One of his favourite sayings was, "When in Rome, do as the Romans." He prided himself on the fact that he could go anywhere and get on with anyone, and he encouraged us to do the same. He used to say to us, "You never know where you are going to find yourself in life, so you have to be prepared." This had been his experience when he arrived in Edinburgh from Malawi with £5 in his pocket. He had embraced the Scottish culture, and in return they had embraced him. He went to great lengths to teach us what knife and fork to use, and exposed us to different foods and wines, so we would not be phased if we found ourselves at a posh dinner party. We would fit in.

I do not have many memories of my friend Lyn at primary school, but she says that I was the only one she bonded with because we were two oddballs, she an "awkward shy introvert Anglo-Indian girl," and me the first black girl in the school. She says initially I was a great source of fascination and distraction to the whole class. She imagined I must have had a tough time, as kids can be so cruel. She says she knew that only too well from her own experience. She says us becoming mates was life-transforming for her. It was us against the world as far as she was concerned. By accepting her as my friend, I gave her confidence she hadn't accessed before and I helped her grow over the years as a person. Looking back, I don't remember any of this, and we never talked about race. I knew Lyn was slightly tanned, but she could have passed for white. I didn't realise she had all this going on. Her brother was much darker than she was.

I remember much more about our relationship at secondary school. We were practically inseparable for the first two years. She lived at the bottom of my road, so every morning I would be ready to cross the road and join her when I saw her coming, and we would walk to the coach stop where we picked up our ride to Wallingford, where our school was. We were lucky if there was a seat on the coach, so we mostly stood. In class, we sat next to each other on the front row in front of our form teacher Mrs Quinn's desk; she also taught us French. We played together at playtimes and we went home together on the coach and we walked home together again. In fact, I had forgotten just how much time we spent together. In class we spurred each other on and we worked well together. I remember Lyn had the most beautiful handwriting, which she prided herself on.

Lyn says she resolved that secondary school was going to be a new start for her and she wasn't going to be shy anymore; she made a point of sticking her hand up to ask questions. As a result of her hard work, she came second in the class exams and went up to 3A in the third year. Talking to her recently, she says she wishes she had stayed in our class as she feels she would have done better and it would have helped her greatly with her confidence. She took a position at the bottom of the new class as the work was harder and faster and she found it very difficult to keep up. Again, I didn't know any of this. I thought she was happy to go and enjoyed her new class and friends. Lyn wishes she had stayed with me, and says I was kind of lucky to have stayed where I was because I didn't have the pressure of being in an 'A' class. And all the time, I was wishing that I had gone up to the A class, because then I would have been with her and my other friend Susan. It just goes to show that we are never happy with our lot as human beings.

At age sixteen, Lyn would have liked to stay on and retake her O Levels (she got to do O Levels rather than CSEs) but her mum insisted she leave school to help with the household bills, because her brother's education was more important. Lyn's mum was the only single mum I knew while growing up. I was lucky my parents didn't insist I get a job at 16 and I was able to delay going to work and pursue my O Levels at college. Even when I started work, I went to evening class to study A Level English. I just had the education bug. But it has been nice while writing this book to have been able to reconnect with Lyn and to be reminded of the special bond we had, which I had very much taken for granted.

By 1988, I was living in South London and had been married for two years, but I was not yet ready to have children. Had I been in Malawi, I would be pregnant within a year of marriage, such was the cultural pressure there. Instead, I chose to do a social science degree at Goldsmiths College in nearby Deptford. At least that way, I would have something behind me. My husband was happy for me to pursue this path and supported me 100%. Social science would not have been my first choice of study – English would have – but the only spare places were on the social sciences course.

There was a huge black section in our cohort. For me, this was the first time I'd been in such a situation. At Oxpens College in Oxford, there had been a few other black people, but not many. To begin with, things were fine and we all got on very well. Then the cohort elected me to be their representative to liaise between the cohort and staff. That's when the problems started for me. I can't quite remember the trigger, but I was accused by the black section of being white. Because I was married to a white man and spoke with an Oxford accent? I don't know. They ostracised me from the first year and it lasted until I left university. It was one of the worst experiences I have ever had. I remember I had read *Hard Times* by Charles Dickens about a man who had been sent to Coventry. I didn't know what that meant, until I was experiencing it for myself. This was not something that Alistair could understand, not having experienced it himself, so he was unable to help me.

The majority of the black group were from the Caribbean. I was African. It was the time of 'Free Nelson Mandela'. A lot of demonstrations were going on in London and boycotts of South African goods until Nelson Mandela was released from prison. The African Caribbean Society, which I was a member of, held a lot of events at that time to highlight his plight, and there was a general feeling that we as black people were all Africans and therefore must stick together. It was a very confusing time for me, because I was the African one, yet I was being silenced. This led me to do a lot of soul searching.

Nelson Mandela was released from prison on 11th February 1990 after being in prison for 27 years because he believed in a free democratic society – one man, one vote – and he wanted the abolition of apartheid. Soon after his release from prison, he made a trip to London to thank the British people for their support of the South African people. My husband bought us tickets, and he and I went to Wembley to glimpse this extraordinary African man who had held the world to ransom and been prepared to die for his beliefs. His story resonated with me greatly. I must add that when I met my husband, he had a huge poster of Nelson Mandela on the wall with the quote at the beginning of the chapter. I would look at him and read it often. On some level of consciousness, I knew that he was inspiring me to be the best version of myself.

In my second year at university, we had to write an extended essay of our choice which would take us up to the end of the third year. Because of the experiences I was having, I chose the title *Black People and Mental Health in Britain*. I wanted to look at the state of my mental health as a black woman growing up in this country. In order to do this, I knew I had to find a black therapist. I must have got this notion from the books that I was reading at the time, such as *Black Skin, White Masks* by Frantz Fanon. So I went on my search. It was not easy, as there were not many black therapists around at the time, but with some detective work, I found a female black therapist at ACMHA (African & Caribbean Mental Health Association) in Brixton. I remember talking to her from a red telephone box to make my first appointment. She saw me privately for six months on a one to one basis. I don't remember her being very expensive.

After six months, she put me in a Black Women's Psychotherapy Group that she was setting up. There were ten of us, and we met every Thursday between 5pm and 6.30pm. If someone left, she would introduce a new person to the group. She would analyse the group, giving an overall description of the vibe within the group. Some people would hog all the time and not leave any time for anyone else to speak. Some people would not speak at all. The group ran organically, in that she didn't steer the discussion in any way. She left us to take what we wanted from it. I found that if you wanted to add to the discussion in the one and a half hours that we had, you had to raise your point before 5.30pm, or else the time would fly by and you'd find yourself fighting to talk. I attended this group for three years, even after I left university and had my daughter. The group was valuable to me because it kickstarted my search for my identity as a black woman growing up in Britain.

I left the group to continue my therapeutic journey with Juliet, who was from the school of thought that if you wanted therapy, it was better to have one to one, not fighting for attention with nine others over a one-and-a-half-hour period. I agreed with her. Also, I had been appalled when one of the Jamaican women had gone to Jamaica and met a man who she brought back to live with her here, and he became violent to the point where she had to sleep with a knife under her mattress. I felt I was better off out of it. When I was with the Black Women's Therapy Group, I used to feel uncomfortable because the facilitator was very much of the notion that we had to support our black men. I was married to a white man. I always knew that I would marry a white man, because living in a village where we were the only black family, the only black men I knew were my dad and my brothers. So I was pleased to leave the group. The group facilitator's boyfriend was mixed race. She was very black. She had the shock of her life when her children were born, and they were white. It just goes to show that you don't choose who you fall in love with.

Reflection

"It's foolish to be obsessed with past failures. And it's just as foolish to be self-satisfied with one's small achievements. The present and the future are what are important, not the past. Those who neglect this spirit of continual striving will start to veer off in a ruinous direction."

Daisaku Ikeda, *Buddhism Day by Day*

We all have to find our own reason why we are here, irrespective of our race, culture or gender. I know my search for my identity on this earth has been long and hard, but I wouldn't change it for a moment. In the end, everything makes sense, everything turns out alright, but we have to be willing to fight for our place. We can all do it; we have everything we need to win this fight within us.

"There is no easy walk to freedom anywhere, and many of us will have to pass through the valley of the shadow of death again and again before we reach the mountaintop of our desires."

Nelson Mandela

Chapter 10:
Jeff's People

"If you are sad, cry. Cry until your tears have washed away all pain. It's like crossing a river of suffering. Those who have done so have a depth and radiance unknown to those who are strangers to such experience. The thing is not to drown in the river."

Daisaku Ikeda

My son James had worked very hard at school, and won himself a place at Durham University to study maths. He said he wanted to do a subject that he loved. Durham had invited him to visit for two days, with accommodation included. He fell in love as soon as he disembarked from the train. He had visited Durham once before as a toddler with his dad, to plant a tree to commemorate his grandmother, who passed away in 1985. His grandparents had lived in Durham and his grandfather taught at the university. On his second visit, students from the various colleges came to the station to meet the guests. They asked them what college they were coming to visit, and then painted their faces with the college colours as they said, "You are one of us now!" This hugely impressed James. He spent the two days there doing activities and meeting lecturers at the maths department. He came home knowing that Durham was where he wanted to go. He had also visited Bath and Bristol, but they did not compare. He wanted to get as far away from London as possible, and Durham fitted the bill. All that was left for him to do was to put his head down and secure his place by getting the required grades. Then his dream would come true.

Durham wanted him to get A*AA, but he got A*AB. The B

was in history, not maths, so they let him in. James loved every single minute that he was at Durham. He worked hard, played hard and made loads of friends. He enjoyed walking to the maths department every morning; his walk took him along the River Weir. He worked at his maths during the day, and in the evenings he went out. He did shifts at the college bar for extra cash and he belonged to various societies. His favourite lecturer was Dr Funke. I thought with a name like Funke, he was Nigerian, but he was of German descent. I remember thinking when I met him at graduation that he was not of this world; but James and his friend Chris would make sure they had front row seats to his every lecture and never missed one in all their four years at Durham.

James' favourite sport was ultimate frisbee, which he loved. I would describe it as a mixture between netball and rugby in that you are not allowed to run when you have the frisbee and you score when the frisbee is passed through two posts. He played frisbee most weekends against the other Durham colleges. When I was visiting him one weekend, I went to watch him train. He was teaching one of his friends how to play. It was the middle of winter, and it was freezing cold. I kept thinking, "I will be the dutiful mother and stick it out watching them play." From where I was standing, it seemed to them that time had stood still. They were so immersed in what they were doing for what must have been two or three hours. When I couldn't take the cold any longer, I took myself into town to find a cafe and to get warm, and James joined me later.

At the university's Jobs Fair, James joined Lloyds Bank because they offered him sweets; jellybeans, to be exact. He was later to regret this impulsive act of accepting sweets from strangers. The summer before he left Durham, he worked for Lloyds Bank in Leeds for ten weeks, to see how he would like it. He seemed to enjoy it. They had put him up in digs with other potential employees. After the summer, he signed a contract for the Graduate Programme to work for them for two years. There were a group of them, all new entries, and they had to do eight months of placements in different cities around the country. James would have liked to go to Edinburgh or Glasgow, but for his first placement, he got Dunfermline. Initially, things were going fine. There was all the excitement of going out into the big wide world after being institutionalised since he was four and a half, and leaving the safe and enjoyable environment of Durham, where he had been exceptionally happy.

He managed to find a house share on a large housing estate in Dunfermline with three other people, two of whom also worked for Lloyds Bank. His work was a 20-minute walk away on an industrial estate. All was going well. However, after the excitement died down, he realised he was not happy there after all. Dunfermline is the sort of place where people stay their whole lives, and hardly any new people moved there, so he stood out like a sore thumb. The housing estate was miles away from the main town. There wasn't anywhere local to go; even buying a pint of milk was a 20-minute walk. The other people in the house had cars, but he was determined to walk everywhere, although there were buses. In Durham, he had prided himself on walking everywhere. He had a few university friends in Edinburgh, where he mainly went at the weekends, as it was half an hour on the train. He didn't really have much in common with his housemates. One of the Lloyd's housemate's main interest was keeping the house spotless; and it was spotless. At work, James had a couple of people he would meet up with for lunch, but it just wasn't what he was used to. Being on an industrial estate, there were no coffee bars or anywhere to go for lunch. Everyone came to work in their cars, and as soon as work finished, they got in their cars and drove off to their already secure lives – that is how it seemed to James. He was pretty miserable.

His best friend was a wind turbine, which he named Jeff. He would walk past Jeff on his way to and from work. He could see Jeff from his bedroom window, and from his office window. He would text his friends and make up imaginary stories about what Jeff was up to. Jeff was his one constant. The only 'person' he was going to miss in Dunfermline when he left was his friend Jeff. He looked forward to his next placement in Glasgow, where he hoped that things would get better, but they didn't. They got worse. He loved Glasgow. With the money he was earning from Lloyds Bank, he was able to find a flat share with another Lloyds Bank employee bang in the centre of town, so all amenities were nearby. In that respect, things were looking up, but he still disliked the job. He decided he hated the corporate world. It just wasn't for him.

I rang him up one day, and he was really depressed. He wouldn't even talk to me, he was that depressed, because he hated his job so much, and he thought this would be the rest of his life. Unlike when he had his face painted when he first arrived in Durham, this time the paint just wouldn't stick. Also, he wasn't using his mathematics, which is what he loved. I was so worried about him. I texted Alistair and said that we needed to talk to James. We had a three-way conversation, and gave him options of other things he could do. He felt he was lacking direction. I suggested he go to Malawi for a few months. His dad suggested taking a year out to travel and some other work he could do instead. We showed him that if he was really unhappy, it was okay to leave. He thought he had signed his life away to Lloyds Bank but this didn't have to be his life.

A few weeks after we spoke to him, he plucked up enough courage to hand his notice in. His colleagues were shocked. "You don't leave!" they said. "Watch me!" was his reply. As part of his contract with Lloyds Bank, he had to pay back the initial signing bonus and compensate them for the training towards a professional qualification, but he was happy to do this if it meant he could leave. He planned to do maths tutoring for A Level students while he sorted out what he was going to do with his life. He never did do the tutoring because around the corner something else was waiting for him, which would have eluded him had he not plucked up the courage to follow his gut instinct and leave Lloyds Bank. Leaving the bank also meant him giving up his flat in the centre of Glasgow and moving to a cheaper flat in the West End, sharing with two girls from Spain and France.

When James moved to Glasgow, the first thing he did was join an ultimate frisbee club. On one particular evening, after work, he was cycling in his rainbow baggy shorts (they wear baggy shorts for frisbee) when he saw another cyclist in front of him, also in baggy shorts. He thought to himself, "I bet he is going to frisbee." So he followed him closely. When they arrived at their destination, he started up a conversation. The guy's name was Alistair, the same name as James' dad. When James asked him what he did, Alistair said he worked for a wind turbine company. "That's cool!" James said.

A few weeks later, Alistair posted on Facebook that his company was hiring. James applied for the job, but he didn't tell Alistair until he got an interview. At this point it was a small company and they did not have a mathematician on board. James said he was going to try and convince them that they should have a mathematician. The interview was very casual. He was taken to a vegan cafe and the two guys interviewing him were casually dressed and very friendly. One of them had studied at Durham. He didn't have to convince them about anything. They were looking to hire mathematicians, as the company was merging with a much bigger company. He also had a Skype interview with the head of HR in Denmark, where the headquarters are based. She said that the company has offices all around the world, and when James had done his five years in Scotland he could work anywhere, if he wanted to. He also learned that the people working for the company were very easy going; they didn't care how you dress as long as you do your job. They were also multinational, so he fitted in very well. In fact, the only Scottish person was their office manager.

The Friday James was going to hear whether or not he had got the job, I was on the fast train going to visit him in Glasgow. At one point, the train came to a complete halt. I looked out of the window and saw a sea of wind turbines swirling round and round, smiling happily at me. Then my mobile rang. It was James to tell me that he had got the job. Unfortunately for him, Jeff's people had beaten him to it. That was rather a profound moment. He told his friends he had a new job; that he was going to be working with Jeff's people.

James decided to take a few weeks' holiday before he started his new job to settle in his new flat and the new office, which was a twenty-minute walk away. When he started, his friend Alistair, who had recommended that he apply for the position, was not in the office, as he was travelling around Australia and Peru. As the company was merging with a much bigger company at this time, they decided to play a prank on Alistair when he returned. They all planned to wear suits and ties on the day he returned and tell him these were the new company rules. Of course, that first day Alistair came in dressed casually. The plan was that the next day Alistair would come in wearing a suit, and they would all be dressed casually and tell him that it was a hoax. The plan backfired rather, because Alistair did not have a suit as all his stuff was stored at his parents' house. I thought it was not a nice joke to play on someone who had helped him to get a job, but James did not agree.

Through his Spanish flat mate, James met his girlfriend Judith, who is from Catalonia; Barcelona, to be precise. She hates to be called Spanish. She teaches Catalan and Spanish at the University of Glasgow. James is now a keen Catalan student. They live together in James' new flat, which he purchased about two years ago. If Judith does not manage to secure her contract to work here next year, they plan to go and live in Barcelona. Like Megan Markle, Judith has come to this country, fallen in love with her prince and is now in the process of stealing him away from everything and everyone he knows and taking him back home to Barcelona with her. Good luck to her, I say. I am busy doing my five minute a day Duolingo Spanish lessons in preparation for when I visit.

Reflection

What was inspiring about James' story was that he had the courage to acknowledge the fact that he was unhappy at Lloyds Bank and, with the encouragement from us, his parents, he was able to take a leap of faith, knowing that there was something far better out there for him – and there was. It was exercising his courage that saved him. It was a good example that sometimes we do lose our way in life, but at the end of the day, only we can get ourselves back on track by listening to our inner voice and admitting that something is amiss and change is needed. James experienced all of that and carved out a new path for himself where he became happy. It required a drop in salary, but his happiness was more important. He put himself in a position where the Universe could assist him going forward and he has never looked back. I am very proud of everything he has achieved. For me, it feels like he is putting into practice everything that I had been teaching him, consciously and unconsciously. He is living the dream.

"You write in order to change the world... If you alter, even by a millimeter, the way people look at reality, then you can change it."

James Baldwin

Chapter 11:
The Day I Tried to Take
My Own Life

*"Everyone seeks the lightness of the future and fears the weight
of the past. Everyone tumbles through the struggle of being here,
playing it out on each other, because it feels too hard to face the
life we're given.
So often we try to flee or silence the tension of being fully here,
which, resisted, is torment, but once accepted awakens us
to a long and nameless dance.
At best, we try to love our way out of it. When that fails, we turn
to violence. If blessed, the struggle enables us
to build, create and serve.
This is why we're here, to be shaped by time into a tool."*

Mark Nepo

I was in one of my depressed episodes. In this state, I would
shut down. I would go into myself, and negativity would set in.
I would no longer believe any of the wonderful things written on
my vision board. I would look back on my life and think how
little I had achieved. I didn't have much to show for it in
material terms. Not that this usually worried me, because I
couldn't do what I was doing if I was worried about material
gains. But when depressed, I would compare myself to my
brothers and my cousins and what they had achieved
materially. Much, much more than I had achieved. What was I
doing with my life? Dreaming of finding something that didn't
even exist.

None of this took away from the fact that I was depressed,
tired and I felt very much alone. This time I was having

suicidal thoughts. These thoughts were real. They would envelope my whole being and stay with me much longer than they should. I had never had them before or since. It was very scary. I didn't want to be here anymore. I thought no one would miss me if I wasn't here. I felt invisible. To me, it seemed that everyone was out there living their lives, having a good time. I felt no one cared if I was alive or dead. When I was consumed with these feelings, I would walk to the railway station with the intention of throwing myself in front of a train. It seemed like a huge jump, which would stop my pain. I thought about going to the shed at the bottom of the garden and staying there until I died. No one would find me there. I would stop eating. That would do it. I remember I even took a bus to Westminster Bridge to see how easy it would be to jump off the bridge. It didn't look that easy at all. This was the first time in my entire life that I felt I would be better off dead. I had always managed to overcome stuff before. I realised it wasn't that easy to end one's life. I mulled it over and over in my head and came to the conclusion that taking pills would be the best way to end my life. I didn't want to be here anymore. I had tried and tried to live my life to the very best of my ability, but I didn't seem to be getting anywhere, or so it seemed. My marriage was over, my kids had both left home, and I had been made redundant. I didn't know what else to do for a job, so it seemed a good thing at the time to end it all.

I went to a few chemists and bought packets of paracetamol and ibuprofen. It was an *EastEnders* night, a Monday or Tuesday. I can't remember if I had dinner. I remember I waited until *EastEnders* was finished, then I went upstairs with my packets of tablets and I took the lot of them with water. I also tried to drink some stuff for unblocking the sink just to finish it off, but it was horrible and stank, so I didn't drink much of it. Then I went to sleep. This must have been eight or nine in the evening and it was March, just before Easter 2014.

I was woken at 4am by horrible stomach pains. They were

so painful I was forced to ring 999. I told the person on the other end of the phone what I had done. She kept me talking on the phone until an ambulance arrived. I remember I could hardly stand. They made me walk to the ambulance. I fell over at one point, and they picked me up abruptly. I had bruises on my arms and face where I fell. They had woken up my lodger to tell her what was happening. I remember being grateful that this had all happened in the night, when everyone was asleep, so I had no neighbours peering at me.

Inside the ambulance, they did a lot of checks before finally driving to the hospital. As it was the early hours of the morning, it was an easy drive up to King's Hospital, and we went immediately to the emergency bay. The ward was very quiet and empty. I was taken to a bed and a nurse started to work on me straight away. I was conscious the whole time, so I was able to watch them as they gave me the antidote to stop the pills I had taken from working. The ward was quiet for hours. I was left alone mostly with my own thoughts. The nurses worked silently and efficiently. I was left feeling embarrassed and ashamed by what I had done. I felt I was wasting their time. I knew I wasn't going to do this again. I stayed in the emergency unit all day while they found a ward to transfer me to. This happened very late in the evening. I was sent to the diabetic ward, as they had found that I was type B diabetic. That was why I had been in physical pain, but I hadn't known what it was. The consultant asked me if I had had any signs that I was diabetic, and I said no. Thinking back though, I had mentioned it to one of the doctors at my local surgery that I was having tingling in my thighs, and he had assured me that it was nothing, so I hadn't taken it any further.

I was taken in a wheelchair to a women's diabetic ward on the third floor. At one point, when the lift doors opened, someone I had worked with on the labour ward was waiting to get into the lift. Fortunately for me, there was no room in the lift, so she had to wait for the next one. I was so pleased, as I didn't want anyone to see me in this state and start asking questions. The ward was full; that's why I had to wait until a bed became available. A very young girl aged about fourteen was in the bed next to mine, but it wasn't a suitable place for her; they hadn't anywhere else to put her. I can't remember what she presented with. Her grandad paid to have her moved to a private ward where she would have her own room. I was pleased, as I didn't want to have to converse with her – or anyone, for that matter. I pretended to be asleep, even when I wasn't.

There was also a woman there who came in for regular cancer treatments. During the five days I was on the ward I was able to talk to her and tell her why I was there. She bought me a toothbrush and toothpaste from the shop as I didn't have anything but the clothes I came in with. They had someone guarding me all night just in case I tried to take my own life again. They wouldn't even let me go to the toilet on my own. This was most embarrassing. There was an older black woman in the bed opposite me who was very sick. Lots of family members and church members visited her. Her son would come early in the morning and feed her breakfast, as they were concerned she was not eating anything. The church members saw how forlorn I was and came to my bedside and said a prayer for me, for which I was grateful. The doctors would come on their ward round and huddle round in a circle near my bed discussing me, before the main consultant would come and talk to me, while the other doctors gathered around me. He would ask me the same questions over and over again: "Why did you do it?" "Did you leave a note?" etc. I kept saying I did it because I just wanted the pain to stop. I was in so much pain.

James was too far away to visit me, but he rang his friend Myles, and he and his mum came. Lonie rang while I was in hospital and I told her what I had done and where I was. She said that her heart had broken into a million little pieces. They moved me to a psychiatric ward because they were worried that I wouldn't be able to cope at home alone and because I was still in shock about my diabetic diagnosis and I had no idea how I was going to cope. On the ward, they would be able to help me with my medication. Lonie came and visited me there with her dad, who waited outside. She bought me an Easter egg, which was sweet of her, but I refused it because I was diabetic now. She had been too scared to visit me alone – who can blame her? – so she had waited until Alistair could bring her. My brother Paul also visited. I merely stared at him while he talked at me and told me I had to get myself out of this place.

I was totally out of it. I didn't have any feelings. I remember I slept a lot as a way of shutting out everything that was going on. And there was a lot going on in that place. I couldn't believe it. You really had to be there to understand. There was so much shouting and screaming, night and day. Lots of women having episodes. My mum and dad had worked in a place like this. Had I chosen to have this experience to better understand theirs? Well, it had worked – and it was an experience I chose not to repeat.

The head of the Home Treatment Team came to see me and offered me visits for up to two weeks when I went home. She said that maybe I could now get rid of the facade. Facade? What facade? I really had no idea what she was talking about, until I had my voluntary lockdown in August 2019, six months before the pandemic lockdown started. Once home, I went back to sleeping all night, then sleeping all day on the sofa. If I wasn't sleeping, I was watching television. My favourite thing to do was sleep, and my favourite time was bedtime. I hoped that I could sleep and never wake up again, because I didn't have to face anything then. Most importantly, I didn't have to face myself. I didn't have to face my life in any shape or form. I knew it was important to eat properly now I had a diabetic diagnosis, so I made sure I went shopping and bought food, cooked it and ate it.

Looking back at that time, that was very strange. I didn't want to be here, but I made sure I ate properly and took my medication. It doesn't make any sense. I was on anti-depressants for a year, as I was so worried that the suicidal thoughts would come back to haunt me, but they didn't and have never come back since. Someone from the Home Treatment Team came every day to visit me. It was a different person every time, which didn't make much sense to me, as there was no continuity of care, but there you have it.

I was by myself again at home, dealing with myself and my life; which junction should I take next, and when should I take it. Slowly, but surely, I started to chant again, and to take each day at a time. I started attending a walking group once a week, organised by the surgery, which was lovely. We would catch a train and go into central London and walk around, or take a train to the countryside and walk there. We would find a nice village pub to stop for lunch. It was important because it was my one constant and it was good to chat to other people and make friends. I met my friend Maureen at walking group. Also, as part of my recovery, I was assigned to see Everest from the Enablement Team for 12 weeks in Camberwell. I would walk there and back through Burgess Park every week to see him and he worked with me on ways of moving forward in my life. I am grateful to him as he showed me kindness and helped me to get back on track. He was a fellow African from Zambia, and an uncle figure. He showed me that, bit by bit, I could get my life back on track and become financially independent, to the point where I didn't need to have a lodger living with me.

When I left hospital, my diagnosis from the consultant was that I had been depressed since childhood. When I told my mum this, she refused to take it on board. I understand that now. For her to have taken that on board meant owning up to her feelings, and I know that would be difficult for her, so I am happy to leave it there. I knew that my life had been saved for a reason, because the consultant at the hospital had told me, emotionally, that they had nearly lost me. But what was the reason that my life had been saved? That has become my life purpose.

Reflection

I have learnt from this experience to pick up the phone and call someone – anyone – and ask for help, before things get too bad. There is always help out there, but you have to ask for it. The one person I felt I could have called was Ranjanie, but she was away for six weeks in Australia visiting family and I didn't think I could bother her. I have also learnt to recognise those times when my vibrational levels are low and take some time out to be by myself quietly, to be in nature, to listen to music, to dance, to do yoga, to chant, to take a walk, to meet a friend, to go and see a movie. There are so many things in my life I can turn to that will make me feel vitalized once again. I count myself one of the lucky ones that I have found my true self.

*"But in the end, one needs more courage to live
than to kill himself."*

Albert Camus, *A Happy Death*

*"It is only through other people's experiences that we learn we
are not the only person on the planet who has sunk to the depths
– and, like the phoenix, has had to find the strength to rise from
those ashes and start again."*

Betty Shine

Chapter 12:
The Day Lonie Died

"I am thinking of Robert, my oldest friend, seven states away. He
understands all of me. There's no translating with Robert. We
knew each other the moment we met.
That was forty years ago.
How will I manage if he should die first? How will I endure the
emptiness his going will open in me? He sees, hears, and
understands without trying. He's the old soul I've found and lost
before. When he goes, he'll pull me into the centre, where I will
have to befriend the emptiness.
Perhaps this is the enduring gift of grief."

Mark Nepo

Lonie died on 6th April 2018. The day before she died, Alistair, her dad, took her to Heathrow Airport so she could catch a flight to Malawi for her cousin's wedding later in the month. She wanted to go early to participate in the pre-celebrations. Her cousin had made her a part of the wedding committee, so she was very excited. I was supposed to be going a week or so later, but I had decided not to go to the wedding. I was worried about the cost, as I didn't have a job and I was still searching for what I wanted to do.

Her dad phoned me to say she had got off alright and how excited she had been, although he did mention that he thought maybe she shouldn't go because she didn't seem well enough. She had been quite ill the week before. But she was having none of it. She was going to her cousin's wedding and nobody was going to stop her. This was the first time her dad had taken her to the airport. Usually I took her. I had tried that morning to lift myself off the bed to go to the airport to say goodbye to her, but my body would not allow me, so I stayed with it. Sometime in February I had come down with depression, and I couldn't move; I spent most of the time in bed sleeping, or sitting on the sofa watching television. I just wanted to shut the world out. I had managed to meet Lonie in Croydon a few times to buy wedding rings for her cousin and get them engraved and to give her money that I owed her for the trip. That was about all that I could manage. The rest she had done alone, or Alistair had helped her.

I remember vividly the day she died. It was a Friday. I was woken by a knock at the door. I wasn't expecting anyone. When I opened the door, it was my friend Anne from the walking group. We had arranged to meet and walk the following week, but she had come a week early. I mentioned this to her, but she shrugged and said as she was here, we should go today. I believe she had been sent by my guides and angels for a reason, so I wouldn't be on my own that day. Anyway, we went for a walk around the cemetery, a beautiful place. At one point we sat on a seat, huddled together, holding hands tightly. I didn't know then, but I believe that's when Lonie died, all those thousands of miles away, high up in an aeroplane between Nairobi and Lilongwe. She was 20 minutes away from her destination. Apparently, she had felt unwell on the plane. At Nairobi, she had been seen by the medical team, who had approved her well enough to fly. They wanted her to stay in Nairobi to have more tests, but she had refused, saying she just wanted to get to Malawi to see her cousin. She had even gone to the duty-free shop and bought some gifts. But she didn't make it to her cousin's. She died on the plane, 20 minutes before reaching Lilongwe Airport. Lonie had created a special Facebook group for her Malawi trip and she had told everyone to come to the airport to meet her. When my cousins learnt that it was Lonie who had passed away on the plane, they told my mum the plane had been delayed and took her home. They only told her the news once they reached home.

Back here, Anne and I had finished our walk and she had returned home. I was sitting on the sofa, probably watching television, I can't remember, when an hour later I received a phone call from my brother Paul to tell me the news. My heart missed a beat as he told me the details. After I had hung up, I rang James and told him. He was at work. He told a work colleague, who said that he must go home, and he personally took him home. Next, I called Alistair. He just so happened to be on his way to Glasgow to visit James, which was good, as James would not be alone that night. I wonder if this was also by divine intervention. I didn't want to tell Alistair while he was driving, but he insisted that I tell him straight away, so I did. He was obviously very shocked, as he had just the day before seen Lonie off at Heathrow. He said he would call me back once he was off the motorway, which he did, and I was able to fill him in with all the details that I knew. I then rang my friend Anne and told her, and she quickly came round to be with me. Rudy, Alistair's friend, came round with flowers. I rang my Buddhist friends and three of them came round with flowers. My friend Sue came round with flowers. My friend Coral came round to be with me. James must have rung her. James' two university friends Katie and Chris came round with flowers. They stayed in the kitchen and organised all the flowers that people were bringing.

My brother Paul came and stayed two nights. People brought food so we wouldn't have to worry about cooking. People came and went. I spoke to my mum, brother and nephews in Malawi. They were all in shock. I phoned people to let them know. I was in a daze. "Why me?" I thought. "Why did I have to be the centre of attention in this way?" Decisions were being made around me about what to do next. It was up to Alistair and me where we wanted her buried. Paul and Alistair took over making the arrangements as I was in no fit state. It was decided that Lonie should be buried in Malawi, at the family farm where my mum's family are buried. So we had to fly to Malawi after all. Although I had decided I didn't want to go to Malawi for the wedding I hadn't cancelled my ticket. Paul, Alistair and James booked on the same flight as me.

I had also notified the family Lonie was lodging with. They were all shocked too, obviously. I met up with the mum, Angela in Costa's in Camberwell. She gave me Lonie's birth certificate and her baptism certificate, which were needed for her burial in Malawi. Angela told me a little story about the two certificates. She had helped Lonie to clean out her room before her travels. They had found the two certificates and Angela had suggested Lonie put them somewhere safe, like the top drawer. This she had done. But after Lonie left, Angela had gone into her room and found the two certificates on the bed. Lonie knew I would be needing them.

Angela said she wanted Lonie's room cleared, because she wanted to let it again, and this upset me. I managed to go with James and Coral and we took as much as we could in the little time we had, before we travelled to Malawi for the funeral. But I would have liked to have had more time to go through Lonie's things properly. That I regret, but there were too many things going on at the time for me to make valid decisions.

I had a premonition that Lonie was going to die. I was walking out of the bathroom into the kitchen one day when this wave came upon me, and I got the message that Lonie was not coming to this house again. It stopped me in my tracks, but I pushed it aside. "What a silly thing to say, that Lonie is not coming back to this house!" I thought, and I shrugged it away as nonsense. Also, that last Christmas Lonie had transferred a lot of her photos onto my computer, so that when my computer was sleeping, her photos would appear one by one on my screen. She didn't say anything, and neither did I when I saw what she had done. It was a silent communication that we both understood. When she left to go home that Christmas, I walked her to the station and said to her that I thought she was trying to tell me something, but I didn't know what. She denied that there was anything wrong. She said she had had a lovely Christmas and she was pleased with all her presents. She had received a lot of presents from family and friends, and I had given her money, because that was what she had asked for. I had worked very hard that Christmas to have a nice time. I had chanted every day for months and done yoga every day as well so that my vibrational levels were high. I am so glad that I did. The last time I saw her alive, she didn't come to the house. We met at Blackbird café, down the road, for a coffee. I gave her money to buy what she wanted, and she came back with a hot chocolate with cream on top. She kept true to herself, and always had what she loved, whether it was good for her or not. She was on her way to visit her godfather. She said she wanted to see all her favourite people before she went to Malawi. She had also seen her English cousins before she travelled. That day, she deliberated on whether she should take the train that was coming now, or the later train, which meant she would be late for her godfather's. I suggested she take the earlier train, so that she was on time. We had a lovely chat, mainly about her upcoming trip to her cousin's wedding. We said goodbye and I wished her a lovely trip to Malawi, as I would not be seeing her for some time. And then she was gone. That was the last time I saw her.

Alistair, Paul, James and I made the same trip that Lonie had made two weeks earlier from Heathrow to Nairobi to Lilongwe. Throughout the trip, my thoughts were that Lonie came past here; we were taking the same route that she had taken. When we flew between Nairobi and Lilongwe, I felt her spirit for the very first time. I knew she was there with me amongst the white clouds and the clear blue sky, welcoming me home to Malawi. I told James and Alistair but they just looked at me as if I was mad.

The funeral started as soon as we arrived at Kamuzu International Airport. I remember my mum and others were at the airport to meet us. Then we were taken straight to the mortuary where Lonie's body lay. There were loads of people there. My cousins had dressed Lonie in the dress and shoes that she had brought to wear for the wedding. They knew because she had posted it on Facebook. Lonie loved Facebook. When I saw her for the very last time, I remember her hair had all frizzed out. She always had it combed back. It was just her body there. The Lonie I knew had gone, but she looked at peace. I stroked her cheek with the back of my hand. I wish that there had been more time to be with her, but there wasn't. I rode with her in the hearse to our village, where she was to be buried, and that was my special time with her. Most of the family are buried there – my grandparents, uncles and cousins. This was also to be Lonie's last resting place; surrounded by her family.

My cousins had made up black clothes for me which were far too big, but I was grateful for them. I hadn't brought any funeral clothes with me. It just hadn't crossed my mind, or had I been told that they were making clothes for me? I cannot remember. Lonie's body was put in the front room where I had lived as a child, and where she had visited for the first time when she was six months old; her first trip to Malawi. The women filled the room, sitting on the floor and singing hymns throughout the night, being there with her. The men gathered outside. That was the custom. At regular intervals, meals were prepared for everyone to eat. I was encouraged to get some sleep in Mum's room next door. James and Alistair went to sleep in a hotel in town. The day of the funeral was going to be very busy; we needed our sleep.

The following morning even more people arrived, and after everyone had had lunch, the church service started. Lonie had been baptised in the Church of England although as an adult she hadn't attended church. The service was in Chichewa, and so were the hymns. I didn't understand much of what was going on. It was a bit of a blur to me. Eventually, we buried Lonie. I hadn't wanted to go at all; I didn't think that I could face it, but I also knew that I had to go and see Lonie one last time. I am glad that I went. Mum and I were the last to leave the graveyard. I told her then that I wasn't coming back to Malawi to live, like so many people were expecting me to. She said she knew.

Our trip was a two week stay, although Alistair left after one week. First, the four of us went to the lake for a couple of days. I was just out of it all, merely going through the motions. Then James, Paul and I went to stay at Mum's in Limbe. Every morning I didn't want to get out of bed; I didn't think there was anything to get out of bed for, but Mum made me. She came and sat on my bed and said to me, "I have lost my husband and my mother, but I still keep going. You just have to keep on going until it's your time. It was Lonie's time, but it is not your time yet."

I ended up staying for the wedding after all. It was a beautiful wedding. The bride looked beautiful, and so did the groom, but I was very much out of it. James seemed to have a good time. I was just glad to get home to London.

When I did get home, I didn't know what to do, so I went back to bed and put the duvet over my head again. This way, I didn't have to think about anything or do anything. I stayed like this until I got the date for the memorial service from Alistair. We were going to have a memorial service for all Lonie's friends and family in the UK. So I had a chat with myself. I wanted to do Lonie proud. She deserved that at least. I couldn't find myself unable to get out of bed on the day of the memorial service – that wouldn't do – so again I turned to my Buddhist practice and started chanting for an hour a day. Nichiren Buddhism states that if you chant *Nam-myoho-renge-kyo* every morning and evening, under any circumstances, you will become happy. I decided to put it to the test. I had nothing to lose and everything to gain.

Because of my chanting, I was able to start organising things for the memorial service so that we could give Lonie a good send-off. It was on 20th June, a beautiful hot sunny day, and many people turned up. Her friends from school, the guides, her friends from college, many of my friends and family, James' friends and Alistair's friends and family. My friend Sue and her mum offered to make all the cakes for the tea, and I was able to organise for some of my Buddhist friends to chant

Nam-myoho-renge-kyo at the end for five minutes for Lonie's eternal life and happiness, and to help her transition to her new life. Afterwards, mostly everyone walked to a venue nearby for tea and cakes. I was more than pleased with how the day had panned out. I knew that Lonie would have been pleased to see so many people there.

I thought after the memorial service I would go back under the duvet again, but I didn't. I continued to get up every day and chant *Nam-myoho-renge-kyo* and do yoga. I started attending The Women's Hub in Peckham, doing various workshops; I also started going to Clean Break in Kentish Town, where I immersed myself in poetry, writing and performing. What was nice about these places were that life had given us a big blow in whatever terms, but as women, we were able to gather together and become creative. It was a time for us to heal.

I also started having therapy sessions in London Bridge once a week. Here, I was given space to talk about Lonie to my heart's content, which is what I wanted to do, as the two people I wanted most to talk to about Lonie – Alistair and James – were not available to me. For that I am very grateful, because it seems that after someone dies, people just expect you to get on with things, when all I really needed was time and space just to be. I didn't have another breakdown until August 2019 when returning from Malawi after my brother Paul's 60th birthday.

This was a reading by our Buddhist president Daisaku Ikeda which Lonie's cousin Isabella read at the memorial service:

Death will come to each of us
Some day. We can die having fought hard for
Our beliefs and convictions, or we can die
Having failed to do so. Since the reality of
Death is the same in either case, isn't it far
Better that we set out on our journey toward
The next existence in high spirits and with

A bright smile on our faces – knowing that in
Everything we did, we did the very best we
Could, thrilling with the thought, "That was truly
An interesting life"?

Reflection

I wrote this poem out on my walk this morning:

Freedom
Everything seems different
It's a new day
I have freedom.

It is three years ago today that Lonie died. I wondered then how I would cope. Life seemed impossible without her. For me, Lonie's death has been the most difficult thing that I have had to endure in my life. I really didn't see it coming, although subconsciously I did know. But, like the quote at the beginning of the chapter, it is her death that has propelled me to the centre and to live my life to the fullest. Her death has taught me the only way to survive is to include her every day in my life, instead of trying to shut her out, which only brings me pain. 'Enduring gift of grief' says to us we must have loved so much to feel such loss. That is the deal we make. It is up to us to carry that love forward and turn it into inspiration to help others who are struggling with loss, because losing someone close to us is universal.

I visited my doctor to tell him about my loss. He refused to put me on antidepressants, advising that I go through the pain. He said this was a call from my daughter for me to get on with my life.

"Suffer what there is to suffer,
enjoy what there is to enjoy.
Regard both suffering and joy as facts of life,
and continue Chanting Nam-myoho-renge-kyo,
no matter what happens.
How could this be anything other than
the boundless joy of The Law?
Strengthen your power of faith more than ever."

Nichiren Daishonin

Chapter 13:
My Cosmic Ordering Stories

"When you learn, teach; when you get, give."

Maya Angelou

From the moment I read Ellen Watts' book, *Cosmic Ordering Made Easier*, I was inspired and started to cosmic order myself. These are some of my orders. Some manifested, some didn't. What I would really like is to do the yoga course with BSY (British School of Yoga), but I don't want to pay anything for it, for the good of all concerned. I made this order in January 2019. I did the yoga course by correspondence, and finished in July 2020, but I ended up paying for it myself by standing order. Maybe I did not look out for the signs once I had made my order, I don't know. But in this instance, my order did not manifest in the way I wanted it to.

In January 2019, I cosmic ordered tickets for *Hamilton*, saying I didn't want to pay anything for them, for the good of all concerned. I didn't get free tickets for *Hamilton*, but I got free tickets for a pantomime, *Snow White*, at the Palladium Theatre in London. My friend Ranjanie had been given the tickets by her daughter, but she was not able to go because she had the flu. On the day of the performance, she asked if I could use them. I said yes and thanked her for them. I immediately rang my friend Lynn and asked her if she wanted to accompany me, and she was able to. It was a lovely performance with a full-studded cast of Dawn French, Nigel Havers, Julian Clary and Gary Wilmot. This was an example of perfect synchronicity, when everything fell into place in a short space of time. I was offered the tickets and immediately, my friend was able to accompany me. There were no hitches. I thanked the Universe. Although it wasn't *Hamilton*, I was aware that I had to thank the Universe, so that more good things could come my way.

Later in the year, I did get my free ticket for *Hamilton* from my son, but alas, I could not use it because I was unwell, but a friend of my son's was already waiting to use it. This teaches us that there's only so much we can plan. We can be ready for the day, but the rest of the time we have to learn to go with the flow.

This is an experience I had of someone who had paid something forward to me. I walked into a card shop in London Bridge with the intention of buying a birthday card for my niece. I picked up a card that I liked and went to the counter to pay for it. On the back of the card, it said someone had paid for it but had forgotten to take it with them. The shopkeeper said I could have it as it had already been paid for. I was delighted and said thank you to the Universe.

When my son moved into his new flat in November 2018, he was worried that he didn't have any furniture to put in it. I put in a cosmic order that he be provided with everything that he needed for the flat for the good of all concerned. He heard from the couple that were selling him the flat that they were happy to leave everything in the flat for him as they were starting afresh, which was great news. Again, I thanked the Universe.

In January 2019, I put in an order that I really wanted to start writing all this down for a book called *On the Road to Living My Life Purpose*. I had shared this with Ellen in February, when I did a workshop with her. Fast forward a year, and I had emailed Ellen to say I was ready to start writing the book that we had talked about a year earlier. The rest is history. I thanked the Universe.

When my husband divorced me, I had to move out of the family home and find a three-bedroom house for the children and me. This was a difficult time for me as I was also dealing with the loss of my marriage. Eventually, I started to search around for somewhere new to live. My only priority was that it be somewhere not too far away so the children could still go to the same school. They were going through enough; I didn't want them to change schools. I found a lovely three-bedroom house on the main road in Nunhead, which was newly refurbished. I put in an offer, but it was declined. The woman selling it wanted the full asking price. Then the estate agent called me to say they had found a buyer for our house, who were keen to move in straight away. I told her I had just looked at a place in Nunhead, but they were asking far too much. She said: "Why don't we go and see that house in Nunhead that I showed you before?" She had not shown me a house in Nunhead before, but I said yes, and was intrigued. The next day she took me to the house I am living in now. I hadn't been here before, but it was perfect for our needs. I put in an offer, which was accepted, and we have been here ever since. I know it was my guides who led me here and I was very grateful and thanked them.

I would really like to be reunited with my brother Peter and his family, for the good of all concerned. We have come a long way with this one. My brother left England with his German girlfriend and went to live in Dusseldorf, had four children, and basically cut himself off from all of us. I would occasionally speak to him on Facebook, and we started to talk more when Lonie died. We eventually moved to WhatsApp, so I could send him photographs easily. One day he sent me a photo of his first daughter blowing out her birthday candles. She was ten. It was such a beautiful photo, I asked him if I could share it with the family group, so that Mum could see it, and he said, "Sure."

Then he asked me who was on the family group and if anyone could join. I told him who was on it – Mum, me, our two other brothers and two nephews – and said that he was welcome to join it if he wanted, as he was family. "Shall I get Sandram, our savvy nephew, to put you on the family group?" I asked him.

"I can do that," he said, and the next morning he was on the family group, conversing with all of us. It just goes to show that everything is to do with timing. The timing has to be right. I have no doubt that one day we will be reunited, when the time is right. I have been taught here that sometimes in cosmic ordering, patience is the key.

One day I found myself dragging my very heavy bicycle to the bicycle shop in Peckham for an MOT, because I hadn't ridden it in a while. I looked around me and could see no one to ask for help, even if I wanted to. I thought to myself, "This is as good a time as any to put in a cosmic order." So I said, "What I would really like is some help with carrying my bike to the bike shop, for the good of all concerned." I looked behind me and walking up behind me was a young black man. I instantly asked him if he could please help me to carry my bike to the bike shop. He was more than happy to assist me, and we had a lovely chat on the way. He went out of his way in delivering the bike right to the shop. I was so grateful, I thanked him profusely, and he went on his way. He had no idea that he was my cosmic order. But it showed that once you place a cosmic order, sometimes it is a good idea to act on it straight away. I had tested this and had been shown instant rewards.

The order that clinched it for me that cosmic ordering really does work is the one about my garden fence that I mentioned earlier. In 2016, while looking down at my garden from my son's bedroom window, I realised that the garden fence looked as if it had not been replaced since the house was built in Victorian times; it also had all sorts of growth on it. I really didn't know where to begin. So I put in a cosmic order there and then: "What I would really like is a brand-new fence, but I don't want to pay anything for it, for the good of all concerned." I wrote the order on the notes page on my phone. Fast forward two years: I was browsing the orders I had written on my phone and came across the order for the fence. I looked down the garden, and there was a brand-new fence. My heart nearly missed a beat. I couldn't believe it. "This stuff really does work!" I said to myself. New people had moved in next door, renovated the house and put up a brand-new fence – and they didn't want any money for it, although we had initially talked about going halves. If I hadn't written down my order, I would never have known that it had manifested, so this showed me the importance of always writing down your orders.

I was forced to make a cosmic order when I found myself stranded at Nairobi Airport in Kenya in October 2018. My brother Paul and I were travelling to Malawi and we were in transit at Nairobi Airport for a few hours. I had put my passport somewhere safe, but when we arrived at our boarding gate, I searched and searched my bag but could not find my passport anywhere. My brother even searched my bag, but he could not find it either. I was beginning to feel very nervous, because without the passport I could not travel anywhere. I thought that maybe I had dropped it where we were sitting, so I traced my steps, but still I could not find it. I went to the information desk to tell them that I couldn't find my passport. She said I had to report it to the immigration office, so I had to walk to another floor where the immigration office was, and they basically told me that without a passport I could not take my flight to Lilongwe. I was distraught. They said I would have to wait in Nairobi Airport until a replacement passport could be sent from London. This could take up to a week.

The call came for the flight to Lilongwe to start boarding, so my brother proceeded to the gate, sad that he could not help me in any way. I went to another desk to seek assistance, but they were also not able to help me. Resigned to the fact that I was now stuck at Nairobi Airport for the unforeseeable future, I sat down on a seat and said to the Universe, "If there is a time that I need your help, it is now. Please show me that this stuff really works." Having said that, I felt calm and started emptying my bag, bit by bit. Right there, sitting in my bag, was my passport. I couldn't believe what I was seeing, and I have never been so happy. But we had emptied my whole bag out and found nothing! Anyway, there was no time to think about that now. I picked up my things, and I tell you, I have never run so fast in my life as I did to the boarding gate. My brother and I were the last to board the plane to Lilongwe. I was so thankful for my cosmic order. No one wants to be stuck at an airport, not knowing when they are going to be rescued. It was an example of calling on cosmic ordering in a time of deep stress.

During lockdown, I was not working. My nanny job had come to an end because families were social distancing, both the parents were working from home and schools were closed, so they had no need for a nanny. The family paid me for three months, so I was able to comfortably be at home. I spent this time doing a lot of yoga and writing my book, so I kept myself very busy. When lockdown was coming to an end, the agency started to send me jobs, but they didn't seem right for me, so I turned them down. A lot of them required that you drive, and I did not want to drive; I hadn't driven in so long. I did have interviews with two families that I thought I would be happy to work with. Both families interviewed me on the phone for over an hour and then invited me into their homes for another hour to meet them and the children I would be working with, but they did not choose me. I was somewhat disappointed, because it takes a lot of time and energy to prepare for an interview.

A little time passed, and I was matched with a new family. The mum talked to me on the phone for about half an hour, and she booked me on the spot. She didn't ask to meet me, or for me to meet the children. She just made up her mind from the conversation we had that I was the right one. I met the family the evening before I started work, and they were lovely. I couldn't wait to begin. They are twenty minutes cycle away. I pick up the youngest girl from school and we go cycling in the park. Then we go home and I help her with her reading and writing. By this time, her older sister, who is at secondary school, is home and the three of us cook supper together and eat it. It is a perfect job for me, just what I ordered from the Universe. On top of that, I get to teach the children yoga, meditation and chanting – which was in the family's job description. I just thank the Universe every day for everything that it is teaching me. I had been asking for a job that I loved, so that I could have time to do the other things I love.

I have also made a cosmic order to meet my soulmate, and to downsize locally from my three-bedroom house to a spacious flat with a small garden and a space where I can teach one-to-one yoga. These two orders have not yet manifested, but I have no doubt that they will, and in the meantime, I am busy looking out for the signposts so that I will not miss my orders when they come.

Reflection

"You must go inside and find the knowledge that the exalted ones were speaking about. It is in and of you, not something they conveyed to you. With your power, you can have that which you seek. You need to put your energy into manifesting. Stop waiting for others to provide for you and bring what you need to yourself now!"

Betty Shine

My cosmic ordering stories have taught me that when we take the time and patience to align ourselves with the Universe, we get exactly what we ask for and more. It has taught me that the Universe really does have my back, but I have to be prepared to take the first step, every time.

Chapter 14:
Buddhism

"What Buddhism teaches us is that only you can write the script of your life. The scenario of your life is not written by some external power; it is not a result of coincidence, nor pre-determined by destiny. You write the story of your life, and you are its star player."

Antwn Owen Hicks, *The Art of Living,* July 2020

I first came across Buddhism when I was 11 years old in Religious Education class at secondary school. I can see Mrs Gee's face now: it was filled with enthusiasm for her subject. She first taught us about Christianity and the story of Jesus of Nazareth. I already knew parts of this story because my primary and secondary schools were Church of England schools, although I had not attended church as a young child. My grandfather had been a church elder, but there came a point when he had to choose between the church and drinking, and he chose the drink. Also, when I came to live in England, neither of my parents went to church, so we did not grow up going to church on Sundays, which for me was a huge advantage because I was able to choose what religion I wanted to follow. Buddhism was what came to fill my heart and imagination. I hung onto Mrs Gee's every word. This religion really resonated with me. We had to do a project on a religion of our choice, but not Christianity or Buddhism, because she had already taught these in class. I chose Shintoism. It wasn't as captivating as Buddhism, but I got top marks and came top of the class. I wonder what mark I would have got had I been able to choose Buddhism. Buddhism ignited something deep in my soul that I had known before.

The next time I came across Buddhism was when I started yoga classes in Benson with Juliet when I was 20, and then, fourteen years later, when I started attending her yoga classes again, where she would lecture about Buddhism for an hour before we practised yoga. For the next twenty years, she gave me the foundation for my yoga and Buddhist practice.

When I met Monica and started chanting in 2014, it was easy for me because I already knew about the teachings of Buddhism. It was the chanting that was new to me, and learning about this particular kind of Buddhism, Nichiren Buddhism. It was only when I started chanting that I felt proud enough to call myself a Buddhist. Before that, I had always cowered away from calling myself anything. Chanting *Nam-moyho-renge-kyo* changed all that for me. I realised that I had two *Introduction to Buddhism* books on my shelf, so I had tried at various times to read the texts, but failed. I guess for me, learning to chant, then reading the text was a much easier way of learning the practice.

The founder of Buddhism, Shakyamuni Buddha (Siddhartha Gautama), lived around 2,500 years ago in Northern India, what is now Nepal. He was born into nobility, a prince of the Shakya tribe, but at an early age he became deeply troubled by what he saw as the four inescapable sufferings of human life: birth, sickness, old age and death. He renounced his life of luxury and embarked on a spiritual search to discover the fundamental cause of, and the solution to, human suffering. For many years he practised some of the extreme austerities and teachings of the various religious sects of those days, but he rejected them all as being incapable of providing the answers to his questions. He realised that he would have to find the solution entirely by himself. He entered into a profound state of meditation under a *bodhi*, or pipal tree, near the town of Gaya in India. There he attained an awakening or enlightenment to the true nature of life and all things, including human suffering. Once he became enlightened, he shared his realization in teachings, which later became texts known as sutras. It was this enlightenment that caused him to be called Buddha, or 'awakened one'.

He resolved to share his understanding so that a more enlightened way to live, in which people were better able to deal with the sufferings of birth and death, would become accessible to more people. His intention was to enable all people to attain the same awakened state of life that he had attained and he spent his life travelling widely throughout the Indian subcontinent, sharing his enlightened wisdom. One of his later teachings was the Lotus Sutra, which is the basis of the School of Buddhism that I follow.

Three key people to have developed Buddhism further, based on the Lotus Sutra, were T'ien-t'ai in China, followed by Dengyo and Nichiren Daishonin in Japan. T'ien-t'ai recognised the importance of the Lotus Sutra in daily life and created the School of Buddhism, basing its teachings on it. Dengyo brought the Lotus Sutra to Japan and founded the Tendai School of Buddhism in Japan. Nichiren came across the Lotus Sutra in a Tendai Temple where he was educated. He further developed the teachings by founding The School of Nichiren Buddhism, focusing on the chanting of *Nam-myoho-renge-kyo,* which SGI (Soka Gakkai International) members practise today. (Myoho-reng-kyo is the title of the Lotus Sutra.) Nichiren was an outspoken critic of the established Buddhist schools and the secular authorities. He also had great warmth and humanity and there is evidence of this in the numerous letters he sent to his followers. He had a deep concern for the welfare of ordinary people, which made him an unrelenting opponent of the often corrupt and oppressive social structures at that time.

Nichiren was born in a small coastal hamlet to a fishing family; these people were of the lowest ranks of the strict social hierarchy of 13th-century Japan. At the age of 12, he began his schooling at a local Tendai temple called Seicho-ji and formally entered the priesthood at the age of 16. He was moved by the plight of ordinary people, which he saw personified in the daily hardships of the people of his village. This concern for human suffering was a profound motivational force in his efforts to grasp the heart of Buddhist doctrine. In one of his letters he describes how, from the time he was a small child, he had prayed 'to become the wisest person in Japan'. Following his entry into the priesthood, Nichiren embarked on a period of intense study of the Buddhist sutras and the various schools of Buddhism, travelling to the major centres of Buddhist learning in Japan.

After a gap of almost seven centuries, the Soka Gakkai emerged as the organisation that would spread the teachings of the Lotus Sutra into eternity. The Soka Gakkai was founded in 1930 by educators Tsunesaburo Makiguchi and his disciple Josei Toda. Makiguchi was already in his late 50s when he encountered Buddhism, and devoted much of his life to educational reform. He came up with a pedagogy based on his belief that the purpose of education was ensuring the happiness of children. In Nichiren Buddhism he found a philosophy that resonated strongly with his own ideas and he revived the original spirit and intent of Nichiren Daishonin, making it relevant for contemporary society.

During World War II, the Japanese militarist government imprisoned President Makiguchi and Josei Toda as 'thought criminals' for their opposition to its policies. Though advanced in age, President Makiguchi carried on his struggle even in prison, asserting the truth of the Daishonin's Buddhism until he died. He passed away in prison on November 18th, 1944.

The second president of the Soka Gakkai, Josei Toda was imprisoned for two years. On his release from prison in 1945, Mr Toda launched a monumental struggle to re-establish the Soka Gakkai, building it into an organisation of almost one million members by the time of his death in 1958.

Daisaku Ikeda, our present president, was 19 years old when he encountered his mentor Josei Toda at a Soka Gakkai discussion meeting. He was instrumental in the post-war development of the Soka Gakkai. In 1960, aged 32, he succeeded Josei Toda as president of the organisation. He took the Soka Gakkai to further development, taking root outside Japan. In 1975, President Ikeda established the Soka Gakkai International (SGI), which now has members in 192 countries and territories.

Nam-moyho-renge-kyo is the fundamental law that pervades the entire universe and all life. *Myoho-renge-kyo* is the full title of the Lotus Sutra in Japanese and literally translates as 'The Lotus Sutra of the wonderful (mystic) Law'. It is called the mystic law because it is difficult to fathom. Chanting *Nam-moyho-renge-kyo* (also known as Daimoku) enables us to bring the qualities of the Buddha to be active in our lives. We carry out our daily practice by reciting a prayer that we call Gongyo, chanting morning and evening to a scroll called The Gohonzon, which is a visual representation of all the forces that affect our lives, which was inscribed by Nichiren Daishonin in 1272.

When we chant, we reveal our greatest potential here and now, regardless of our circumstances, whether we be rich or poor. I look at it as a gift to chant every morning and evening. It is a time when I can be with my own thoughts and reflect on what is going on in my life. I often do my 'To do list' while chanting and, when finished, I happily slip into my day knowing that I am able to deal with anything that the Universe is going to throw at me. I feel well protected. I am connecting with the Universe and the ancestors before me, asking them for advice and wisdom, and it is a comforting feeling. If I don't chant, I feel that there is something missing in my life and I find that my day will not go as smoothly.

You usually hear about chanting by word of mouth, like I did from my friend Monica, or you may be invited by a friend or someone you know to a discussion meeting in your local area, which takes place once a month. Discussion meetings are geared towards newcomers who want to learn more about Nichiren Buddhism. Beginning to chant is easy. All you need to do is put your hands in front of you in the prayer position and chant *Nam-myoho-renge-kyo* continuously. At the beginning, it is recommended that you chant for five minutes and increase it slowly as time goes by. The discussion meetings take place in each other's houses. Some meetings take place at the local Buddhist Centre, which for me is Brixton. Our National Centre is in Taplow Court, near Maidenhead. People come from all around the world to chant at the National Centre. At the meetings, we support each other and share experiences of what we are going through in our lives, be they good or bad. We encourage each other through adversity and share the common goal of never giving up on our dreams. Impossible is nothing. We also subscribe to a monthly magazine called *The Art of Living*, which I have quoted from in this book.

I have tried and tested that by chanting *Nam-myoho-renge-kyo*, you can overcome all adversity and suffering. I did this when Lonie died. I learnt to come out of my depression and chant for her happiness in her new life, thus helping her transition. I have learnt that our loved one's soul stays around us for a while, before moving on, to see how we are coping with their departure, and they of course will be saddened if we cannot let them go. Our fellow Soka Gakkai members will chant for our happiness when we have problems, which is very reassuring on this life journey. You are never alone. Chanting *Nam-myoho-renge-kyo* with a lion's roar and taking action with this powerful life force means we can overcome any deadlock. Nichiren Daishonin says, "One who abides by the Lotus Sutra will inevitably attain Buddhahood." (The writings of Nichiren Daishonin, Vol. 1, p779.)

We strive earnestly to help others revitalise their lives by what we call 'turning poison into medicine', encouraging others to do their 'human revolution', which is their greatest challenge. For me, my human revolution has been writing this book. We learn that the greater the challenge or hardship we have to go through, the more we are able to expand our life state and become extremely happy. That is why I love Buddhism so much.

Reflection

These are the readings that gave me inspiration this week:

*"It is not a question of your environment or those around you,
nor what the organization or leaders may be like. To be swayed
by such externals is pointless. It all comes down to one person:
you. What matters is that you become a brilliant beacon, shining
with joy and happiness, and live your life with confidence and
courage.
If you shine with a radiant light, there can be no darkness in
your life."*

Daisaku Ikeda

And...

*"It is important to remember that your worth as a person is not
based on your profession. It is not based on wealth, fame or
academic credentials.
What counts is how hard you have striven in your chosen path,
how much good you have accomplished, how earnestly you have
devoted your energies to it.
It is your spirit of devotion, your sincerity,
that determines your true worth.*

Daisaku Ikeda

The reason I decided to write this book was to heal the
relationship with my mum, which had always been strained
because of the anger that I still harboured towards her because
she had left me in Malawi as a child while she came to England
to pursue her education and to build a better life for my
brothers and me. I had done that now, and in week thirteen of
my book writing, she chose to take her leave and passed on. It
was as if my writing this book gave her permission to go. Her

work here was done. I was not broken by her passing like I had been with Lonie's, because I continued to chant *Nam-myoho-renge-kyo* and my life carried on. I knew I had to finish this book, in memory of her. I knew that is what she would have wanted me to do.

"Chanting daimoku is the foundation of the Daishonin's Buddhism. When we chant sonorous daimoku, the sun rises in our hearts. We are filled with power. Compassion wells forth. Our lives are lit with joy. Our wisdom shines. All Buddhas and Buddhist deities throughout the universe go to work on our behalf. Life becomes exhilarating."

Daisaku Ikeda

Chapter 15:
A Time to Heal

"The entire purpose of life here on earth is for people to be free.
We spend precious time fighting with one another as to the right
way to fight for the freedom we want. Women want to be free.
Men say they want to be free. We will never be free as long as we
need something or someone else to give it to us."

Iyanla Vanzant

Apart from my anger, which was the trigger for me to write this book, I have also suffered a lot from fear and loneliness. I guess the three are very closely related. The anger feeds the fear, which feeds the loneliness. Where did it all start, I wonder? Growing up, I chose to be born into an African society where women's voices were not heard. Then, as a young girl, I travelled to a land where I had the opportunity to have a voice and to grow in any way I wanted – something that would not have happened had I stayed in Malawi. As a child, I remember always getting into trouble for having a strong opinion of my own. I remember having a disagreement with my dad when I was about 9 or 10 and him chasing me up the street. I cannot quite remember whether he caught me or not, but that was the pattern. My brothers wondered why I was choosing all the time to get into disagreements with our parents. It was easy for them. They would just listen to what the parents had to say, and when they had heard enough, they would merely walk out of the room and shut the door behind them. Not me. I would stay and argue and give my point of view, which was always unique to me. I guess I knew from a very young age that I was going to have to fight for what I wanted. I saw how unfair the world was towards women. In Malawi, while living with our grandparents, Grandad came home one evening with some whistle sweets and gave one to each of the boys. They were ecstatic and went somewhere up the hill and blew their whistle sweets and sucked them 'til dusk. I wasn't allowed a whistle sweet because I was a girl. Grandad had another bag of ordinary sweets. He would give me one; I would disappear somewhere quiet and suck it until it was finished, and then I would appear again and ask him for another one. My grandad was a big man, and although I was his favourite, being his only granddaughter, I was also quite scared of him, so me begging for another sweet involved me peeping my head around the corner until he caught sight of me and beckoned me to come in. Then I would take another sweet, and run away again and hide.

When my Uncle Hobson was getting married, I was to be a bridesmaid. But I was dropped because they couldn't find another girl the same size as me. In the end, I didn't even attend the wedding. I was left at the house to mind some other children with runny noses who didn't stop screaming because they missed their parents. I was a mere child myself. I was sure this situation would not have arisen had my mum been there to fight my corner.

When I first went to school in Malawi, one of my uncles gave me a beautiful pencil with a rubber at one end. Well, the boy sitting next to me in class snatched the pencil out of my hand, broke it in half and gave me the half without the rubber. That was what my life was like and I never told anybody, but kept the hurt and anger inside myself. These early experiences taught me that I had to work extra hard if I was to succeed in this male-dominated environment. This was my training ground, where I learnt to be angry, fearful and lonely; where I tried to escape from the male-dominated world in which I lived.

I learnt to be angry because I felt I wasn't listened to; I didn't have a voice. I learnt fear by not being able to express myself and my feelings, and this led to my loneliness, shutting myself away and not speaking because I didn't believe there was anyone who wanted to listen to what I had to say. This was indeed a very lonely place.

When I started having therapy sessions in my thirties, and was for the first time in the presence of someone who really wanted to hear what I had to say, what I was feeling, I was aware that so much damage had already been done, and that the roots of my anger, fear and loneliness were so deep that it would probably take many lifetimes to unearth them, but I had to start somewhere, and in this lifetime.

This is an extract from my diary on 31st December 2019, when I was in the depths of depression.

"Why do I feel like this? Why do I feel like it's me against everyone? I feel no one loves me. No one cares about me. No one would care if I wasn't here. I have no purpose, no reason to be here. In fact, I don't want to be here. I hate everyone, I don't want to speak to anyone. I don't answer my phone or return texts. This is what happened in August, September, October, November, December, January. Today is actually 31st December, Brexit Day. Today was the first day that I felt like a new person, or today was the first time I felt the old Maggie coming back. Today I felt there was hope. So for the last six months, I have been a recluse. I wouldn't go outside; I slept most of the time, and when I wasn't sleeping, I was watching television, because then I wouldn't have to think. I just stared at it. I watched others having wonderful lives, or should I say they were portrayed as having lovely lives. Isn't that what television does so well? Everyone is having a better time than you.

This time, I chose to let my depression ride its own course. I blamed everyone else for everything that was wrong in my life, and at these times, there was plenty wrong. This is so unlike me because usually I am, in my mum's words, 'happy go lucky'. I couldn't wait to go to bed, to get some sleep. To sleep it all away. All those horrible hurtful memories that I endured as a child. They all come tumbling down on me, reminding me of the pain I went through, where there was no one to comfort me.

I was all alone. I wasn't close to my mother. I blamed her for leaving me. She couldn't be bothered with an ungrateful child, which, looking back, I really was. So it was a stalemate.

After a night's sleep, I couldn't get up in the morning. I didn't want to get up and out of bed, because that would mean having to face the day, and that I didn't want to do. I had nowhere that I wanted to go. I had no one that I wanted to see or be with, because they would detect the state I was in and that it wasn't the status quo. I had gone far beyond that. I was ashamed. I feared this to be my cycle now. Bed, television, eat, bed... I didn't go to the doctor and get some pills. I had been down that road before. I also didn't have the energy to walk to the surgery, or I didn't want to. For me, I did the best thing and let the dark cloud pass over me on its way to wherever. Nothing or no one meant anything to me. I just wanted to be left alone. I saw other people bounce back from situations in their lives. What was wrong with me that I couldn't? I didn't know. I just wanted to sleep and watch television, period. My favourite programme was *Escape to the Country*, at 3pm, where I would watch couples escaping the busyness of London and heading for the hills, the sea and the stunning views. How jealous I felt, but I also loved watching them all, for they all seemed happy.

I even gave up chanting. There didn't seem to be any point. Everything exhausted me. I had chanted three times in six months and I really didn't want anyone coming round and telling me that I should chant and that it would be good for me, so I refused to answer texts or let anyone in. I didn't want to read anything that Daisaku Ikeda had to say. I was bored of it.

Over the years, I had become an expert at raising my vibrational levels and reaching the divine – but why couldn't I stay there? I wanted to stay there. Why was I still gravitating towards the pain? After thirty years of searching for the formula, you would have thought that I would have found it by now, but that was far from the truth. Every time I found my mind had travelled to a painful memory, I would quickly reverse it to a happy memory, then consciously jump to another happy memory, or think of someone I loved, and how good they made me feel when in their company, or think of something funny they had said. This I would do until I fell asleep exhausted, for it was hard work turning my negative thoughts into positive thoughts.

Even at these dark times, I would wake up from a lovely dream more times than from a bad dream, and this confused me, but also gave me hope. I felt held by a universal love – that was my goal, until I remembered everything else. Then my heart would miss a beat, and I would be back to my love/hate relationship with my mum. When my life is going well, I am grateful for all that she has done for me. When I am under a cloud, I blame her for absolutely everything. I knew that was no way to behave, but why do I behave like this? Why do I not take responsibility for all of my life? Why can I not grow up? Will I continue to blame her to her grave? Is there a cure? What will the relationship with my mum turn out like? Will she die in this state? What chance did Lonie have with all this encircling hate I was turning onto myself? After six months inside myself, what can I create on the outside? I was scared of everything. I didn't think there was a way out for me. I didn't trust myself to say 'yes' to a job because I didn't know whether I would be able to turn up or not.

I knew that I had to get away from the victim mentality. The memories and the knowing were always there, the good and the bad, and I knew on some level that remembering all my memories was my destiny.

I had remembered that we are spiritual beings having a human experience. We come from a soul family or group whom we have shared hundreds and thousands of lifetimes with. Before we are born, we ask the souls we choose as our parents and other members of our extended family for the lessons that we want to learn this lifetime and we ask them to help us achieve these lessons. When we come to earth, we suffer from amnesia and we forget why we came here. Instead of seeing ourselves as the all-loving, powerful, intelligent, incredible souls that we are, we choose the victim stance and thus spiral down into negativity, bogging ourselves down. We create a fractured story for ourselves, which we keep replaying again and again, until we give up the will to live.

I remembered back when I was in the psychiatric hospital, the Home Treatment Team leader said to me, "Now maybe you can get rid of your facade." I didn't know what she meant then, but I certainly did now. I came across the fractured story concept in Simon Hassa's book, *Yoga and the Dark Night of the Soul*, in which he explains that the dark night of the soul is what we experience when the fractured story that we have been carrying around with us reaches a point where it can no longer sustain us, and we reach breaking point. In the dark night of the soul, our life story as we know it gets shattered. We learn that our personal story is not who we are. Much of it has been inherited from our family, friends, our culture, our schooling and environment so that we feel a sense of belonging. It has been handed down to us unknowingly over the generations. We suffer the dark night of the soul as a reaction, and this gives us the opportunity to rewrite our story how we want it written, with love and affection. Some call this 'coming home'. If the opportunity is taken, it is the ultimate spiritual lesson on the journey of the soul. I started to learn to choose what energies, thoughts and influences I allowed into my consciousness. I learnt to become aware of lower energies that were around me and affecting me. I came to realise that this awareness was ongoing and required my attention for the rest of my life.

For me, meeting my dark night of my soul was life changing, as it is meant to be. Coming out of my depression, I started to chant and do yoga every day. Due to Covid-19, I had lost my job and was back to square one, jobless with the question, "How am I going to stop myself from becoming depressed over lockdown?" I had started a yoga course the previous year with the intention of healing my life. Lockdown gave me the opportunity to do three sessions of yoga a day on Zoom. At the same time, I was reading *Yoga and the Dark*

Night of the Soul and keeping a diary, as I had a lot of emotional pain surfacing from all the yoga I was doing. I was digging really deep, but I felt I had no choice. I felt I had to keep going or die. There was no going back for me. And then something shifted for me. I noticed that I became happier; I had more energy and I started to enjoy the situation I found myself in. When I finished my 150 hours of yoga for my course, which didn't take long, I wondered what to do next, and was led to writing my life story, which is something that I have always wanted to do, again as a way of healing.

The time had come for me to heal my life.

"Humans have difficulty going day to day without anticipating some reward for the negativity they have to live through. They do not realise that accomplishment of understanding the test is the reward they sought before they became human."

The Masters of the Spirit World

Reflection

I knew that once I had finished this chapter, my story was complete. The story that I wanted to share at this moment in my life, because as we know, life is always changing, and that is the beauty of it. Nothing stays the same for long. I had come a long way; from anger, depression and despair to truly knowing love, gratitude and forgiveness for everything that I had learnt and to everyone that I had forgiven. I am truly on my way to living my life purpose and living the life I came to live this lifetime. And to top it all, I have the privilege of sharing what I have learnt with those who are ready to listen, and I understand that not everybody is ready.

My Grandmother

This is a piece I was compelled to write when my grandma died on 19th June 2014. I know there is repetition here, but I wanted to keep it as I had written it.

~~~

My grandmother died a few weeks ago. She was my mother. She raised me until I was eight years old. She is the only mother that I can recollect while growing up. My real mother left me when I was eighteen months old to go and join my father, who was already in England.

My grandmother was my whole world. I vividly remember her clothing me, feeding me; she strapped me to her back while she tended her crops. I followed her everywhere. She was always there for me.

My grandmother had twelve children of her own. And she looked after my two brothers and me. She never complained. That was not her style. She just got on with it.

My uncles and aunts would often tell me when we saw a plane going above that my mum had gone in an aeroplane to a faraway place called England, and that one day she was coming back for me. I was quite puzzled and really could not understand why my mother would want to go to a faraway place called England instead of being with me; why she would choose to be with my dad rather than be with me.

My brothers and I were not treated differently, but we knew we were different. Every so often, a photographer with a huge camera on sticks would come to the house to take photographs of my brothers and me to send to my parents in England. I would scream the place down and run away because I was not having my photograph taken for her who had left me.

I was so angry with my mother.

My father sent money so we could be educated in a European school. He sent beautiful material so I could have beautiful dresses made. Once my mother sent me a beautiful white doll, with flickering eye lashes, a beautiful dress and exquisite shoes. I tore that doll up into shreds, because I was so angry with her for leaving me. She wasn't going to get away with it that lightly.

My grandfather and his two brothers had come from South Africa and bought land a mile or so from each other, built brick houses (not huts like the local villagers) and become farmers. My grandparents were very much looked up to by the villagers. My grandfather's job was in town where he resided during the week, and at weekends he would always come to the farm. He had a government job recruiting for the mines in South Africa. My grandmother ran the farm and we all helped her. There was always something to do on the farm, even for a minor like me.

In the warm evenings, we would eat outside in the compound. My grandmother was the sort of person who, if anyone was passing the compound while we were eating (and they usually were), would insist they washed their hands and share our food. My little mind would be thinking: "But there is hardly enough food for us!" but there you have it.

One day my father sent me the most ugly thick grey material I had ever seen in my entire life. My grandfather explained that my two brothers and I were going to England, and where we were going was very cold; we would need to wear this material to keep us warm. Well, I cried and cried and cried. Was I crying because of the ugly grey cloth, or because I was going to England, or because I was leaving my grandmother, my whole world, for the unknown? I really don't know.

But what I do know is that my leaving broke my grandmother's heart.

My grandmother travelled with my brothers and me from Lilongwe to Blantyre, where we were to fly to England. On the five-hour coach journey, she gave us hot chicken and rice (my favourite food in the whole wide world), to the envious looks of everyone on the crowded bus. This time, she did not insist that we share.

She stayed with us for months and months at my uncle's house, while we awaited clearance from President Banda to leave the country, until one day she announced that she couldn't stay away from her farm any longer. She had to get back to her other family and responsibilities. I am sure that that too broke her heart, for she desperately wanted to see her grandchildren get on that plane with her own eyes.

As for me, I didn't care where I went as long as my two big brothers were by my side. And I was going up in that big mighty aeroplane. To England, to meet my mother.

Grandma, I just want to say that you were the best mother a girl could ever want, and that I love you very much.

Reflection

Reading this story back after some years have passed, I am reminded of the deep love and affection that I shared with my grandmother. I was truly loved and cared for. It makes me understand that yes, my mum left me, but she left me in the capable hands of her parents, whom she trusted implicitly. I will always love you, Grandma, for the careful way you took care of me.

Dear Mum

On 1st June 2020, I started to write this book because I wanted to mend our relationship, which, as you know, has not always been easy. I was able to share with you my plans and we spent many an hour over lockdown talking about my book on WhatsApp. I know you were proud of me. You have always been proud of me, although sometimes I didn't understand why.

On the 13th week, just as I was about to start writing Chapter 13, you passed away. It was a sad moment for all of us, especially because it seemed we had come full circle and we were finally at ease with one another.

I am so glad that I started to write this book. It has given me clarity about my life; about loving and letting go when the time comes, treasuring all the lovely memories and even turning the bad memories into cherished moments, because it was in those moments that my life was shaped. I did not know you, Mum, until I was eight years old, and the contracts we made to come and support each other this lifetime were deep and painful, I would say for the both of us. It has taken me sixty years to unravel our relationship, but I am so glad that I did.

You were my mum. You always knew who you were, where you came from and where you were going, and you instilled that sense of pride in all of us. All four of us have it. You knew England was not your home. You had some place else in your soul that you wanted to be. That was Malawi. You worked very hard at your job; you sacrificed everything for a better life for your children. And when the time came, you were happy to leave the life that you had built here and return home to your beloved Malawi. You took care of your mum – Grandma – until she passed on and, being the first born, you took up the responsibilities in the family. That was your life purpose. I could never compare to you in a million years, however hard I try. But I can carve my own path, the path I was born to live, and for that I am so grateful for the burden you bore so I could be free. You were the wind beneath my wings.

It is ten months now since you left us, and we still don't know when it will be safe for us to fly to Malawi and pay our last respects to you. For me, I know you are with me everywhere I go. I feel you every day, in the wind on my face, in the trees when I am out walking; I hear you in the birdsong. You are protecting me every step of the way, and I shall be eternally grateful for that because your wisdom is entrenched in me always. I want to thank you, Mum, for agreeing to be my mum this lifetime, and for all the lessons that you have taught me along the way. Yes, Louise Hay was right when she said we choose our parents. I couldn't have chosen a better mum.

    With love from your daughter,

    Margaret x

Reflection

Writing this letter to my mum on the soul plain has made me realise that we are all here on Planet Earth for a short time and each of us will return home to plan our next adventure when our soul is ready. Losing a mother makes this realisation all very imminent, because I am now next in line. It was not very long ago that I felt well cushioned because my grandmother was alive; so was my mother and Lonie. Now I am the last female in this blood line. The question for me is: what am I going to do with the rest of my days? I now know that with the rest of my life, I will continue to help other people learn how to live their life purpose. I am certain of that.

Conclusion

*"Amazing things happen when
a prepared person and an opportunity collide."*

Ellen Watts

As I was preparing to write the conclusion, I came across the above quote in Ellen Watts' book, *Cosmic Ordering Made Easier*. Then I came across this piece of writing that I had written in my diary at the beginning of 2020 as I was coming out of my depression:

"In my time of need I so desperately wanted to talk to someone. I ended up talking to myself. And in those dark moments I listened to my voice. I heard that I had a voice. All these years I have been waiting for someone to unleash me. Little did I know that I had everything that I needed deeply embedded within me, waiting, waiting for the right moment, which only I knew. The guilt has gone. I no longer feel responsible for anyone but myself.

"When I finally came out of my depression and opened my mail, there was nothing untoward there. The bank letters had been for my information only, just acknowledging my circumstances and wondering when I would be able to release some funds. I was able to start again where I had left off. The fear had all been in vain. There had been no bailiffs knocking on the door threatening to take stuff away, like you see on the television, and I didn't have to do time in Her Majesty's prison."

Looking back at my diary, I see that writing this book had been a cosmic order that I made in January 2018, but that year things took a difficult turn when I lost my daughter. It was two years later, in 2020, that my book came to fruition. The death of a child changes your life forever. Life takes on a new urgency to live each moment to the full. It's like I am living life now for the both of us, and there is not a moment to waste.

I have learnt to heal my life by living life at my pace. I am not in competition with anyone else. I am a unique soul and I have come this lifetime to discover who I am as a divine soul and to carry out my mission, which is to guide other souls who are stuck to realize their life purpose. I thank everyone who has helped me on my journey, be it big or small. I ask myself frequently why Lonie could not be here with me to enjoy what I know now. Then I remember that she is here with me; it's just that I can't see her. I couldn't have done this journey without her. This is the pact we made before becoming human. I understand that now.

I wasn't one for travelling and seeing different countries. The only travelling I wanted to do was travelling inside myself. I wanted to get to know my soul. What was the point of travelling to faraway places with myself, whom I didn't like very much? Much better to stay home and get to know myself better.

I was out walking with my friend yesterday in the May sunshine, when we came across a local bookshop. I said to my friend, "Just let me go in and ask if they will stock my book once it is published." The lovely man behind the counter – another Alastair – said he would happily take two books to see how it sells and to let him know nearer the time and he will hold an event for me. I was surprised how easy it was once you got to the mountaintop. How easy it was for people to just take over and sell my wares. I somehow thought it was going to be as difficult as the book was to write But I was wrong. I had already done the hard work in the writing of the book.

I am enormously grateful to everyone for this opportunity to tell my story.

I have been keeping a diary for 30 years. I was given the privilege to write about me, something I had always wanted to do. I wanted to write about my life and how I had experienced it. I became aware that Ellen doesn't accept everyone who comes to her wanting to write a book. Recently, when the enormity of what I had done dawned on me, I asked her why she had chosen me. She simply replied, "Because I felt you had a story to tell."

When I had finished writing the book and it was at the beta reader stage (when the book is sent out to various people, some I know and some I do not know, for feedback), I thought it would be a good idea to send a copy to Juliet, my first mentor, who had started me off on my journey all those years ago. I had lost touch with her when she retired, but I found her husband John's e-mail and sent him the book to give to Juliet for her perusal, as she had never been one for technology. He e-mailed me back a few days later with the news that she passed away on 8th March 2019. I was devastated by this news and am still processing it. Looking back, I had googled her name about a year ago and found an entry saying she had passed away and mentioning her husband John and that she left four children. My mind didn't take it in. "It can't be her," I'd thought. I concluded there must be another Juliet in the village with the same name as her, with a husband called John and four children. I refused to take it in and carried on with life until John e-mailed me the news. It just goes to show how our mind can distance itself from things that it is not yet ready to embrace, because doing so would be too painful. So, all the time that I had been writing the book, she was in heaven, probably helping me from up there like she always did. I am just glad that I have been able to express what a beautiful soul she was and to keep her memory alive.

Finally, Alistair and I have just had the pleasure of announcing the engagement of our son James to his girlfriend Judith.

~~~

I had this dream a couple of days ago, while taking an afternoon nap: *I am working with a whole load of people on a production in this huge building with high rafters. I am sitting up in bed. This man, who is half-dressed with a shirt on and a good body, comes and opens the huge window next to me and exposes a beautiful sunset. He asks me if it's okay to leave the window open, and I say, "Of course." Then everyone goes out for the break and I am left alone on the bed, relaxing. Then an old pipe breaks above me and starts pouring dirty water onto the clean white sheets on the bed next to mine. A dirty Victorian-like doll falls down on the bed. An arm of a girl with pigtails appears from the ceiling and grabs the doll and disappears. Waking up from my sleep, I realise that I am surrounded with so many other characters from past generations, most of them theatre people. It's like the film "The Others" with Nicole Kidman, when they realise that they have been sharing their house with generations of people who have passed on. I am so scared, I run down the stairs as fast as I can to join the others to tell them about what I have just seen. I am scared out of my wits. This can't be happening. In my haste, I come out of the wrong exist and I have to walk around the building to where the others are to tell them my news.*

I woke up abruptly. Wow, what a dream. It was amazing, as I had just finished delving into the past by writing my book.

"What fine qualities and superior points do great people hold in common? Ultimately, isn't it that they have successfully challenged and overcome their own weaknesses and persevered until they achieved their desired goals?"

Daisaku Ikeda

~~~

"Buying our souls back can be an expensive and time-consuming process. Coming back into alignment can hurt for a while. But the time, money, emotional energy and effort we put into freeing our souls will be the best energy and money we've ever spent."

Melody Beattie

About Me

The catalyst for me writing this book was wanting to heal the anger that I had harboured inside me since childhood; especially for my mum, who had left me as a child in Malawi while she came to Britain with my dad to make a better life for us. She was now 81 years old, and I did not want her to go to her grave with me being angry at her. The journey of writing this book took me ten months, and I can say that during that time my anger has been totally eradicated.

The most difficult part about writing this book was dealing with the anger that I had for the family I grew up in. When it came to editing it was very difficult because I had to relive the anger again. What was I going to leave in? What was I going to take out? I also had to come to the realisation that this was real; the fact that it was going to be published. I remember my coach saying that a lot of people would shelve it at this point, and I totally understood. I too could have easily shelved it because it was just too tough. I am writing about me, my life and my feelings; real people will be reading it; my relationships will change, or have changed already. Was I ready for all of that?

My hope for the book is that people will like it, that they will take something from it and that it will help them on their path to their life purpose, whatever that may be.

When I am not writing, I enjoy going for walks with friends. My favourite place to walk is Nunhead Cemetery. I enjoy doing yoga, swimming and I love cycling around my local area. I like writing in my diary and reading spiritual books; I belong to a women's writing circle at Clean Break. I am also an after-school nanny to two lovely girls, Ottilie and Allegra. I have lived in London for over 30 years and I presently live by myself in Nunhead.

Contact Details

Website:	www.livingyourlifepurpose
Email:	maggie.kaipahmilne@sky.com
Twitter:	@maggieKaipah
Instagram:	@maggiekaipah-milne
Facebook:	Maggie Milne
	Livingyourlifepurpose

Further Reading

Your Soul's Plan – Robert Schwartz

Cosmic Ordering Made Easier – Ellen Watts

What to Say When You Talk to Your Self – Shad Helmstetter

Living Magically – Gill Edwards

The Power of Now – Eckhart Tolle

Yoga and the Dark Night of the Soul – Simon Haas

You Can Heal Your Life – Louise L Hay

Soul Journey – Lisa Cherry

Memories, Dreams, Reflections – C G Jung

Making Love to God – Tina Louise Spalding

Healing the Shame that Binds You – John Bradshaw

Feel the Fear and Do It Anyway – Susan Jeffers

The Artist's Way – Julia Cameron

The Celestine Prophecy – James Redfield

The Road Less Travelled – M Scott-Peck

Wake up to Yoga – Lyn Marshall

Beginnings of Learning – Krishnamurti

Journey to the Heart – Melody Beattie

Finding Your Way Home – Melody Beattie

One Day My Soul Just Opened Up – Iyanla Vanzant

Anatomy of the Spirit – Caroline Myss PhD

Why People Don't Heal and How They Can – Caroline Myss PhD

For Today and Tomorrow: Daily Encouragement – Daisaku Ikeda

You Were Not Born to Suffer – Blake Bauer

The Boy who Saw True – Published by The C.W. Daniel Company Ltd

Buddhism Day by Day – Daisaku Ikeda

Things That Join the Sea and the Sky – Mark Nepo

The Art of Living – Buddhist magazine

Further information about Buddhism also available from www.sgi-uk.org.

Printed in Great Britain
by Amazon

81447243R00108